So Tales
The Fireside Stories

Hollis L. Green

Coffee Table Books
an imprint of GreenWine Family Books

So Tales

Copyright © 2012 by Hollis L. Green

Library of Congress Control Number: 2012934704

Green, Hollis L. 1933 —
So Tales
The Fireside Stories
ISBN 978-1-935434-58-0

Subject Codes and Description: 1) HUM015000 Humor: Form-Anecdotes and Quotations 2) FAM019000 Family and Relationships: Family Relationships 3) HUM012000 Humor: Topic-Relationships

Printed in Australia, Brazil, France, Germany, Italy, Spain, UK, and USA.

Book Cover Design by Barton Green

Author Photo by Carie Burchfield-Ofori: cariephoto@gmail.com

The Press does not have ownership of the contents of a book; this is the author's work and the author owns the copyright. All theories, concepts, constructs, and perspectives are those of the author and not necessarily the Press. They are presented for open and free discussion of the issues involved. All comments and feedback should be directed to the Email: [comments4author@aol.com] and the comments will be forwarded to the author for response.

Published by
Coffee Table Books
an imprint of GreenWine Family Books
a division of GlobalEdAdvance Press

www.gea-books.com

So Tales
**Is affectionately dedicated
To the descendants of**

Herbert Barton Green
(January 8, 1907 - October 8, 1937)
&
Grace Curton Green
(February 11, 1905 - May 4, 1996)

Five Grandsons
Robert Danny Stout, Sr. (1947-)
George Dewey Stout, Jr. (1952-)
Barton Lynn Green (1956-)
Brian Lane Green (1962-)
Gibran Jackson Faust (1965-)

Three Granddaughters
Janice Elaine [Stout] Henson (1950-)
Myra Sue [Stout] Therber (1957-)
Vanessa Wren [Faust] McPherson (1961-)

Five Great Grandsons
Robert Danny Stout, Jr. (1969-)
Heath Barton Stout (1975-)
Nathan Alan Henson (1981-)
Kyle Yoshia Shimonaka (1986-)
Joel Saburo Shimonaka (1990-)

Three Great Granddaughters
Rhonda Gail (Henson) Banasiak (1975-)
Lindsay Brooke (Therber) Adkins (1985-)
Ashley Nicole Therber (1987-)

Two Great-Great Grandsons
Allister Reed Banasiak (2005-)
Ethan Robert Stout (2009-)

So Tales

Contents

PROLOGUE

Hollis L. Green, Th.D., Ph.D., is a one-of-a-kind man, the likes of which may never be seen again. Just as Hollis writes about Pastor Smith in his So Tales, "Isn't it good that God made a few special people to make life exciting?" So, too, we can raise the question in reference to Hollis L. Green.

The collection of wit, wisdom, and humor reveals a Southern lad with English roots who grew up hard, who missed his father dearly, and who was surrounded by a loving family. Yet because of his early years, Hollis developed sensitivity and insight so useful to his ministry through education.

Many of the So Tales reflect a hint of tragedy, yet the lessons taught (often by family and friends) have shaped a man who is humorous, engaging, thoughtful, and creative. It takes talent to derive philosophy from the daily lessons experienced by a small child, a youthful minister, and a man who shares his world for future generations so openly.

The readers will find the So Tales a "good read." Moreover, they will meet a new friend, Hollis L. Green. Although the meeting may never be face-to-face, the readers will empathize with the author and absorb these little tales into the fabric of their lives.

—Margaret M. Sullivan, PhD,
Regional Chancellor, University of South Florida

PREFACE

Hollis L. Green, ThD, PhD, Founder and past Chancellor of Oxford Graduate School (www.ogs.edu) and OASIS UNIVERSITY (www.oasisedu.org), is a master story-teller. So Tales is a collection of anecdotes drawn from a lifetime of keen observation of the human condition. Each of the true stories from his reminiscences offers a lesson of practical value written in a way that is both enjoyable and easy to remember. Readers are telling us how So Tales brings pleasure twice: the enjoyment of laughter and pleasure upon the first reading, and then in the second reading, the appreciation of valuable lessons in living as the principles illustrated in the short narratives take application in their own lives.

Those who know Dr. Green will love him more deeply after reading these personal insights; those who meet him first in these pages are in for a delightful new experience.

—Richard P. Walters, PhD
Former Dean, Oxford Graduate School

Author's Introduction

Through the years, when I repeated an anecdote or used a funny story in the pulpit, my mother, wanting to know if the story were true, would ask, "Is that a so tale?" A few years ago I was telling a "so tale" and my son, Barton, the writer, said, "Dad, write those stories down." The volumes of SO TALES are a result of that injunction.

Significant events in my life are characterized by biographical humor presented as documentation for other members of the family. The episodes are, hopefully, presented with ingenuity and verbal skill sufficient to evoke laughter and serious reflection. This volume groups the stories into four sections: 1. Grandparents, Childhood, and Cousins; 2. Courtship, Marriage, and Relatives; 3. Domestic and Foreign Travel; and 4. Preachers and the Ministry. At times the same story may teach different lessons and were repeated to make a different point.

Sit down with a cup of fresh brew and enjoy. Hopefully they are all in good taste and will add some comic relief to your life.

—Hollis L. Green, ThD, PhD

SECTION ONE

Grandparents, Childhood, and Cousins

1   YOUR SINS WILL FIND YOU OUT

My cousin, Donald Pogue, and I wanted to go swimming, but were told we had to replant a corn field before we could leave. We were given a bucket of seed corn and told it would be enough to replant all the corn that didn't come up. As the day got hotter and the urge to go swimming increased, we decided to dig one large hole and eliminate the bucket of seed corn all in one spot. The urge to go swimming blocked all the possibility of consequences.

A few days passed, and we wanted another favor from Grandfather Green. He told us if we could explain a phenomenon he had observed in the corn field he certainly would oblige us. Taken to the corn field and asked for an explanation for multiple sprouts of corn coming from one hole at the end of a row, with many blank spots still in the corn rows, I answered, "We ran out of seed corn and asked God to provide for the rest of the field. I guess God misunderstood and put it all in one place. The next time we need God's help, we'll be more specific."

Grandfather responded, "The next time you need help is right now. You better start praying!" We were grounded but learned a valuable lesson about telling the truth and fulfilling obligations. Oh, we learned something about consequences, too!

2   HAWKS WON'T GET THE CHICKENS

One summer, my older sister, Betty Jo, was staying with Grandmother Green and trying to get her to go somewhere. Grandmother said she couldn't go because the hawks might get her chickens. Misunderstanding or just not knowing the difference between a hawk and a hollyhock, my sister took a hoe and chopped down all of grandmother's beautiful hollyhock flowers.

Rushing in Betty Jo exclaimed, "We can go now, the hawks won't get your chickens 'cause I cut them all down!" Grandmother's measured response to my sister's sincere effort was a lesson in patience with a child. She liked flowers, but she loved grandchildren more. I wish all parents and grandparents were as patient as Grandmother Green. The world and all the children would be much better. The adults would be happier, too!

3 DON'T KILL ANY DEAD SNAKES

On one of the annual fishing/camping trips to Piney Creek, I became ill. Probably it was some of the camp stew (I think it had bugs in it), or I was just tired. It was suggested by one of my uncles that I remain in camp and rest and that if I felt better I could gather some wood and perhaps fish off of the big rock nearby. They left a single shot 22 caliber rifle and some fishing gear with instructions to watch out for snakes and not to shoot up the creek. If I had to shoot, I was to be sure it was down the way the creek was flowing so the bullet wouldn't ricochet and hit one of them. My Uncle Edward had killed a snake and put it in a place where I was sure to discover it. It was a set up!

I did feel better later in the morning and decided to fish a little. Loading the single shot rifle and gathering the fishing gear, I headed for the big rock. To get to the big rock you had to jump to several smaller rocks and then jump to the big one which was out in the creek. This I did, but as I was ready to take the last jump I saw a snake coiled on the rock. I took the rifle, checked the safety, aimed, and killed the snake dead. How do I know I killed it? When I shot the snake, it quivered and fell into the creek and floated away—dead.

At the camp supper I was asked how my day went and was told that they had heard a shot. I explained that it was to shoot a snake on the big rock. They all began to laugh and told me that one of them had killed the snake earlier and coiled it on the rock. I protested that it was alive because when I shot it the snake wiggled into the water. They tried to tell me that it was the snake's nerves. Naturally, I didn't believe them because I had seen the snake move after it was shot. I didn't even know snakes had nerves. Oh, well, kids never win such arguments, but grown-ups should be ashamed when they play tricks on kids. That's the way I feel about it!

The big family joke for years was, "Hollis, killed a dead snake!" I guess I'll never live it down. What if I really did kill that snake, and they are just pulling my leg? The truth will probably never come out; it's too good a joke on me! Come to think of it, each time I killed a snake, I never told anybody. I just didn't want the hassle. All my uncles who played that trick on me are gone now, so I can now tell my side: "I killed that snake "graveyard dead" fair and square and I am absolutely positive about it. Nobody alive can prove different, so I got the final say, HA! HA!

4   "THERE'S A DAM BOAT"

Taking my two small nephews, Kyle and Joel, on a joy ride in a jeep, they asked me to tell them a story. Driving toward a dam on the Tennessee River, I chose to make up a tale. "Now, this is the dam road, and these are the dam people, and this is the dam bridge, and that's the dam water, etc...." The youngest screamed, "There's a damn boat!" I remembered my Uncle "Dub" Curton pulled that one on me, and Mother got upset with the additions to my vocabulary.

The same thing happened a few weeks later when the boys were riding with their grandmother and came to a dam. You guessed it: they went off on the same "story" I had told them, and their grandmother came down on them hard for such foul words. They said it was true because Uncle Hollis had told them about all that damn stuff.

5   DINOSAURS WERE HERE

Riding along, my young nephews began to ask questions about the countryside. I told them it was dinosaur country. One asked, "How do you know that?" The other exclaimed, "The dinosaurs are all dead!" Seeing large rolls of baled hay in the field, I told them it was dinosaur doo-doo and that the power poles and wires were really fences to keep dinosaurs off the road, etc.

A few weeks later riding with their mother, the young one shouted, "There's some dinosaur doo-doo." His mother asked, "Where did you hear such a thing!" The answer was clear and confident, "Uncle Hollis. He knows everything!" I guess we all should be careful what we say to children. When they learn bad stuff from adults the consequences come down on them.

6   A LESSON FROM LITTLE LEAGUE

In Vacation Bible School one summer the children were singing, "If you are saved and you know it, say AMEN!" One little blonde girl was singing, "If you are SAFE, etc." The teacher attempted to correct the child, but with no success. Her brother was a star in the Little League, and she understood "safe." She had never been lost and didn't understand the concept of being "saved."

Later while preparing a Sunday sermon, I discovered the word "saved" meant "to make safe." Perhaps the little girl was correct; she was happy because she felt "safe." From the mouth of a child came a lesson learned, not in Sunday school or church, but from Little League. Early sports participation has real value for all members of the family, especially the younger siblings of the ones on the team.

7   YOU'RE A CHICKEN THIEF

At Graysville Elementary School one of the teachers had a scheme to exchange eggs for candy and then sell the eggs to buy athletic equipment. This meant that all the school children were bringing eggs to school from many sources. Me and Cousin Donald Pogue decided to get rich so we gathered all the eggs from my Grandfather Green's barn and hen house and hid them by the gate.

The next morning on the way to school we stopped to pick up our loot and were discovered by Grandfather. He promptly marched us to the corn crib, cutting down a sassafras bush on the way. While he beat his pants leg with the bush, Grandfather called us chicken thieves. I insisted that we stole no chickens, just took some eggs to exchange for candy.

Grandfather firmly informed us, "There's a chicken in each egg. You steal an egg; you steal a chicken." He never laid a hand on us, but the value of the lesson was heavy on our hearts for years. Even today I often wonder, "If you take a paper clip, do you steal an office?" "If someone stole an apple, are they guilty of stealing an orchard?" Perhaps children should learn a few more lessons from grandparents.

8   I KNEW I WOULD GO TO HELL

When I was a child, my paternal grandparents would wait until the water in the rain barrels froze and then make ice cream. One cold winter evening we waited for the ice to freeze in the rain barrels. It was late when the ice cream was ready, and I ate too much too fast. My stomach became hard, and I chilled. My Grandfather made some special coffee for me to drink. He secretly put a little whiskey in the coffee. Later, when a cousin told me, I just knew I would go straight to hell for drinking whiskey. Grandfather Green explained to me the medicinal properties of good whiskey and the negative results of abuse. I never took up whiskey drinking, but I did get hooked on ice cream.

9   ABOUT TO PERISH TO DEATH

One of Grandfather Curton's truck drivers, Vester Dobbs, stopped by my house one day very hungry. He said, "Gracie, I'm about to perish to death. I could eat a horse." That sounded funny to me. I believe Vester was my mother's cousin. Mother told him she had nothing to eat and that she was about to go to the store for groceries. All she had was a box of graham crackers that the ants got into, and she had put the box in the garbage.

Vester said, "Lorde be, Gracie, give me them graham crackers. Them ants ain't got bones big enough to hurt me." As a boy, each time I heard a big truck coming, I hoped it was Vester. He was something else to see and hear. There are not any more of his kind left in the world - at least not in Tennessee to my knowledge!

10   TATER PIE

As a child, sweet potato pie was my favorite, but I hated pumpkin pie. One day my grandmother made pumpkin pies, and they looked and smelled just like sweet potato pie. I ate a piece and have been able to tolerate pumpkin pie ever since, but sweet potato pie remains my favorite. Taste buds are amazing things; they can adapt to almost anything if it's sweet enough. I enjoy all kinds of pies, but still prefer sweet potato pie!

My uncle, Thomas Heneger Green, shared this personal story: As a young man he went to Chattanooga to look for work and decided to drink some coffee and eat a piece of pie. He sat down at the counter in a small shop and ordered coffee and pie. The waitress asked, "What kind of pie do you want?" He answered, "Tater pie! What else kind are they?" I guess his mother had lots of sweet potatoes.

11   MY CROP OF SWEET POTATOES

My Grandfather Green set aside a small piece of ground for me and told me I could plant anything I wanted on it. Since I love sweet potato pie, the decision was to plant sweet potatoes. The ground was prepared, the plants secured, planted, and watered. I waited with hoe in hand. Each day I inspected the rows for weeds and if one was present I chopped it down to the roots. My diligence was overkill.

I did not understand the law of diminishing returns. The more I chopped weeds, the smaller the potato hill became; consequently, there was little dirt left in the hill in which the potatoes could "make." There should have been about 12 bushels of sweet potatoes at harvest, but I had less than one bushel. Grandmother Green made me a sweet potato pie, and I sold about 20 cents worth at the Farmer's Market.

I changed the coins into pennies and added a few nuts and washers to my pocket to make it look and sound like lots of money. It wasn't much money for a summer's work, but I learned a lot...I think! The main thing was that one can overwork a garden and I guess lots of other things. The pie grandmother made sure was good. It was the fruit of my own labor, not counting Grandmother's cooking. She cooked on an old wood stove, and her kitchen always smelled wonderful.

12   SMOKING RABBIT TOBACCO

My cousin Donald Pogue and I used to smoke rabbit
tobacco. It grows wild and has long, thin, grey leaves that
burn slowly. One day Donald and I were hiding in the middle
of a sage grass field smoking rabbit tobacco when one of us
dropped a match, and the field began to burn. Soon it was
out of control and all I knew to do was run and call for help.

I actually said, "Donald set the field on fire!" Later
I justified my accusation by saying I brought the rabbit
tobacco and Donald brought the matches. Since they were
his matches,... he caused the fire. Of course, no one but
Donald's father blamed him. Years later I recanted; Donald
appreciated my confession, but said it really didn't do him
any good since his father couldn't hear it!

I guess it's the "child" in us that wants to blame someone
other than ourselves for the mess we make of things. It
is all an effort to avoid the logical consequences of our
behavior. My mother had her own definition for excuses, and
she was not very tolerant of them. Her definition was, "An
excuse is the skin off a reason stuffed with a lie." When
I see rabbit tobacco growing wild, it always reminds me of
that day and how easy it was to blame someone else to avoid
consequences for my behavior. As a child it was always hard
to accept responsibility for my actions. Sometimes, it is the
same as an adult.

13   BABY RUTH CANDY BARS

I do remember one more story about my Grandfather
Curton. Each time he visited my home at 316 Ziegler
Street, Chattanooga, Tennessee, he would bring candy.
Knowing I liked Baby Ruth candy bars, he brought me a sack
full. I thought Baby Ruth candy was named for the famous

baseball player, but later learned that it was named after the daughter of President Cleveland, baby Ruth, who was born in the White House.

In those days a Baby Ruth cost a penny, and it was about the size of a 75 cent candy bar today. I ate the whole sack full of Baby Ruth's, all twenty-five, and got sick. Yea, there are consequences even to eating candy. I guess I got what Mother called "foundered" on Baby Ruth's. After that episode, I generally choose a PAYDAY Bar or Snickers. Eating twenty-five Baby Ruth's can sure mess up your appetite for candy bars for a few days. Grandfather Curton never brought me candy again!

14   CHRISTMAS AT GRANDMA'S

I remember Christmas at Grandmother Green's house. There was a real live tree taken from a field close by and decorated with stringed popcorn, the fire burning, popcorn balls, apple cider, and lots of fruit, nuts, and candy canes. What more could a young boy want? Grandmother liked peppermint sticks, and would hang a few peppermint candy canes on the tree. They always managed to have things under the tree for me. They were small gifts, but they sent a strong message of love and caring.

I would sleep in a back room with no heat. Before going to bed, I was told to bake my back before the fire. This I would do until my PJ's would burn my skin. Then I would run as fast as I could and jump in bed. Grandmother's beds always had so many quilts that once you were in bed and covered up you had to stay in that position. The cover was just too heavy for a child to turn over. The sheets were ice cold, but the back baking before the fire made the cold sheets tolerable. When one feels loved, it is easy to sleep. These are good memories.

15   BACKLOG ON THE FIRE

It was a joy to watch my Grandfather Green tend the fire in the winter. He fine tuned it, as if he were an engineer. Before going to bed he would put a large backlog at the rear of the fireplace and move the fire around until it was burning well. Then he would take a shovel and put ashes over the fire until it was almost smothered out. It would just simmer. In this manner the fire would burn slowly throughout the night and still be there the next morning.

One morning I was up early. It was cold, but I observed my Grandfather reworking the fire for the morning. It was almost out. He had walked across the floor on the sides of his feet. After raking off some of the ashes, he reached into the chip box and put a handful of small wood chips on the hot coals. He then bent over and blew two or three big breaths on the coals and chips until they ignited. Then he ran back to his bed in the corner and stayed until the room got warm, well a little warmer.

He enjoyed sitting by the morning fire in a small straight-back chair, smoking his pipe. Those are good memories. If I joined him by the morning fire, he never talked, but he would always reach over and rub my head and shoulders. It made me feel so wanted and loved. Present day parents could learn a few lessons from the old folks. I guess keeping a fire burning taught the old folks some things about people and relationships, too. One must work at both or the fire goes out!

16   MY FIRST DAY AT SCHOOL

I began school in 1938 at age 5, a few months after my father died. I walked three miles to Graysville down a narrow road. It seemed like the end of the world. I was one who always wanted to be at home, now I would be in a crowd of strangers.   Arriving on the school grounds some of the older boys began to pick on me. Looking into my hair, one said, "This boy has ancestors." Another looked down my back and declared to everyone, "This boy has garments on his back." The recent sudden death of my father had caused me to be overly concerned about illness. Disturbed that I may have some incurable disease, I never stayed at school, but walked the three miles back home.

Mother was surprised to see me and asked why I was home. I asked her if I had ancestors and she said, "Yes." Then, I asked her if I had garments on my back. The answer again was, "Yes." I went to the bedroom and sat down on the floor. Later, Mother, wondering where I had gone, began searching for me.   When she found me on the floor, she asked, "What are you doing?" My answer was simply, "I'm waiting to die." With this statement, Mother ask some questions about what happened at school. She realized the problem and explained to me that I was not sick. The boys were just playing a joke on me. I never did like people who played jokes on kids! Still don't!

17   THE OLD PIPE TAUGHT A LESSON

My Grandfather Green grew his own tobacco and smoked a pipe. I used to sit close to him while fishing because his pipe smoking kept the bugs away. One day Donald Pogue and I were caught smoking corn silks or rabbit tobacco, I don't remember exactly. But I do remember what Granddaddy said, "You boys are old enough for the real thing." He selected his oldest pipe and strongest tobacco,(which he saved for just such an occasion) and sat us down on the front steps. We were told to smoke the pipe like a man.

After a few puffs, we were both "green around the gills," but Granddaddy insisted that if we continued puffing, the sick feeling would go away. So we huffed and puffed until we were too sick to puff. It was Granddaddy's way of saying to us, "You are not ready for manly things."

Once we recovered, we continued being boys for a while. The lesson of the old pipe worked. I finally became a man, but I never did take up smoking. To this day even second-hand smoke makes me sick. I guess that is a good thing. It saves a few dollars and protects my health. Like most non-smokers, I think smokers are rude without realizing it. What if I ate pure garlic and blew fumes into their face? I doubt they would appreciate my lack of social grace.

18   SAVED ME MANY A SACK OF FLOUR

My Uncle William lived up a steep hill with a narrow road that was often washed out. He did not own a car so it was not graded or kept automobile ready. The family walked up the hill. Others drove a mule and wagon, but no one in an automobile would attempt it because of the ruts in the road.

Still Uncle William would constantly invite people to come for Sunday dinner knowing they would have to park at the bottom of the hill and walk up in their Sunday clothes. At Sunday dinner, especially when his guests didn't choose to make the climb up the hill, Uncle William would often say something about it. His favorite comment was, "That hill has saved me many a sack of flour!"

Gail and I now live one mile farther up that road on top of Lone Mountain. Since my Social Security check is small because of so many years on "missionary stipend," I suppose living up this road could save me a few biscuits. Perhaps I should not fix the road too good, and it may save me some gravy, too!

However, sometimes I get "people fatigue" working so closely with church members and graduate students. Since the road is passable, to get a little peace and quiet, I have been thinking about placing a sign at the bottom of the hill to limit the traffic. What would the sign say? Out of many good suggestions, I am considering the following:

"TRESPASSERS WILL BE SHOT.

SURVIVORS WILL BE PROSECUTED."

--By order of the Sheriff of Nottingham--

The plan included pouring some red paint on the ground, shooting holes in a couple of trees, and placing some "yellow crime scene tape" on the trees to make the sign believable. But I decided against this approach. Everyone is welcome! You know what you like to eat so bring it with you, and we will help you eat it. Doesn't that sound fair?

19   ONE FOR YOU, ONE FOR ME, AND ONE FOR GOD

My father, Herbert Barton Green, (1907-1937) was a deacon in the Mountain Creek Baptist Church when he died. Many years later, I met a friend of his who told me about Barton's last night at church. It seems they took up the offering and went to a back room to count it. Daddy began the count, "One for you, one for me, and one for God." It was just his way of making a mundane task a joy. His Plan B was to "Throw all the money up and ask God to take what He wanted. All that came down would be for the counters."

My father died the next day, but his sense of humor lived on in the heart of a friend. It is important to recount good memories, especially to those who were young at the time. Pass it on.

20   THE STOLEN POCKETKNIFE

When I was about ten years old, Mother bought me a pair
of boots that had a pocket knife in a little holder on the side
of the right boot. Somehow I lost the little pocketknife.
After searching everywhere, I still could not find it. I went
to the Dime Store near the end of Market Street Bridge and
looked at the pocket knives. Having an empty knife holder
on my boot, but no money, I just looked at the knives and
priced each one. During the process, I tried one in my boot
for size, and something came over me, that I could just walk
out of the store with the knife in my boot and no one would
ever know. This I did. It is the first time I remember
stealing anything.

All the way home, my wounded conscience dealt with me.
The next day I returned to the store and replaced the knife,
but didn't say anything to the store people. My conscience
still was not satisfied.

The next day I returned to the manager and told him what
I had done. He asked me to show him the knife. This I
did, and he said since I had been honest about it, he would
let it slide. He also said he would put the little knife up for
me and keep it until I got the money. I had a nickel so I
gave it to him and returned each week until the little knife
was paid for and was really mine.

Through the years I have often thanked God for my
conscience and for the store keeper who understood the need
of a little boy to have a knife, especially when his boot had a
knife pocket. It is a good thing to trust children when their
heart is right.

21   HI, FRANCES!

During World War II my Aunt Ree and Uncle Nick Pogue moved to Charleston, SC, to work in the ship yards. My cousin Frances and I loved Aunt Ree and wanted to visit. The families agreed we could ride the Greyhound Bus from Chattanooga to Charleston. We were at the station early and secured the front seat. I sat by the window, and Frances, a teenager about to blossom, sat on the aisle. It was a good trip. We both enjoyed the scenery, but had one perplexing problem.

As we neared Charleston, sailors returning to base began to board at almost every stop. As the sailors climbed the inside stairs on the bus and caught a glimpse of Frances, they would each say, "Hi, Frances!" We could not figure it out. How did they know her name? We began to offer each other different explanations, but none of them seemed to explain how they all knew her name.

Explaining the problem to Uncle Nick, he simply said, "Well, Frances, you have your name right there on your tit!" Frances wore a pink sweater that showed her early development, and above her left breast she had a gold filigree pin that simply said "Frances." At last, the riddle was solved. Obviously, the sailors were more mature and noticed what we could not see.

Looking back, it was wonderful to be innocent and enjoy life without having to deal with the sexual implications of even a small name pin on a pink sweater. Things sure have changed. Have you seen the ads, the billboards, and the commercials? For the sake of the next generation, I wish someone would do something, cause I'm getting bug-eyed looking at all this stuff!

22   GHOST SAILORS IN CHARLESTON

During my visit to Charleston, SC, during WWII, my cousin Donald Pogue took me to the movies. Walking to the theater, he told me that "ghost sailors" walked the streets of Charleston at night. He said they were the crews of all the sunken ships and that they took liberty at night and walked the streets of Charleston. Just the thought made me scared. The movie was scary, too.

Following the movie, Donald began to say, "Hurry, we must get home because it's getting dark. You know what I told you about those dead sailors that roam the streets at night." With this reinforcement, Donald said, "Let's take a shortcut; it's getting late." Down an ally we went. It was dark. Suddenly, Donald grabbed me and pulled me into a doorway. He said, "Here come some of those ghost sailors." I could see them. I could see their white uniforms and white hats, but I could see no hands or faces. It was scary. I stood silently peeping around Donald, not even breathing. Sure enough it was sailors on liberty . . . black sailors. Their uniforms were visible, but because of the dark alley their faces and hands were not. It appeared to be empty uniforms marching in the darkness.

It was a good joke on me, but I was really scared. I tried to be brave, but a ten year old in a big city believes things they are told. There ought to be a law against scaring kids half to death . . . especially during war time! I promised that if Donald ever had a son, I would scare the "heebie-jeebies" out of him the first chance I had. [The rest of the story: by the time I met his son, he was too big to scare!]

23   A HUNTING DOG GOT OUR FOOD

When I was a young man, I taught a Boys Sunday school class of ages 9-11. I promised those who attended each class for eight weeks a camping trip. Nine boys qualified for the trip. A man from the church drove us to my Grandfather Green's place. There we borrowed a horse and a sled and loaded our gear on the sled and walked behind it up Lone Mountain. In the vicinity of a mineral spring we set up camp.

As the camp leader, I hung our food by a rope in a tree to protect it from the animals. With everything secure, we hiked off to see the sights and returned tired and hungry to a scene none of us would ever forget. A large hunting dog was able to jump high enough to tear the bottom out of the food sack. All the bacon was gone and most everything else was contaminated.

Two of us hiked off the mountain to "borrow" a few items from my grandmother. We made it through supper and breakfast, but with no food the desire for camping was over. We loaded the remaining gear on the sled and went down the mountain. The camping trip may not have been successful, but it was memorable. Those nine boys still remember the lessons learned through my inexperience. I learned a few lessons, too!

24   DONALD PREFERRED THE OLD FORD

The summer of 1943 was spent on my Uncle Blucher Curton's farm at Yellow Creek in Rhea County, Tennessee. There I learned to drive his farm tractor and do other things a small boy of ten could do. I was most intrigued by my cousin Donald Curton, who was about to go off to war to become a fighter pilot. He had the most unique request of his father which was to take the old stick shift '36 Ford on a date instead of the new column shift '41 Ford.

Since Donald was his only son and about to go off to war, Uncle Blucher would approve each of his requests. Later, I asked why he wanted to drive the old Ford. His explanation further confused me. He said, "It is too hard to make a mistake with the column shift." It wasn't until I got my first old car, a '39 Plymouth Coupe, that I finally understood. One evening driving my girlfriend home, my hand slipped off the gear shift and landed on her knee. Suddenly, it dawned on me why Donald wanted to drive the old Ford. I guess we learn some things indirectly even if not on purpose.

25   BOLOGNA IN THE LETTER

My sister, Betty Jo, wrote a boyfriend, John C. Vineyard, during World War II. She would do her homework, write a letter, pray over it, and go to sleep. This she did night after night for several years.   Mother constantly reminded her not to put any "Bologna in your letters." "Remember, John C. is fighting for the country and doesn't have time for foolishness."

One day she was looking for a letter from John C., but could not find one. She asked, "Did anyone see the mail? Did I get a letter?" My sister Sue answered, "It's in the icebox." Betty Jo responded, **"In the icebox!"** The answer was simple and logical, "I put it in the icebox so the bologna wouldn't spoil."   Mother's instruction, Betty Jo's diligent writing, and Wilma Sue's innocence combined to make for a big family joke. Once after that, Betty's letter was served on a plate between sliced bread. She didn't think her bologna sandwich was a bit funny, but everyone else did!

After four years of writing letters, John C. came home from the war, but there was no marriage. He seemed like family, more like a brother than a boyfriend. In fact, John C. did marry and so did Betty Jo, but not to each other; however, both couples remained friendly, almost family. John C. passed, but his wife and Betty maintain a long friendship. I guess that B.O.L.O.G.N.A. had some first names: John, Jean, Betty and George. It was pretty good stuff!

26 CCC DOCTOR PULLED MY TOOTH

When I was a small boy, my maternal Grandparents lived in Reliance, Tennessee, in an old commissary which they used as a company store for their saw mill business. In the middle of the night I had a terrible toothache (are there any other kind?), but there was no dentist in the rural area. Nothing my Grandfather Curton could do would stop the pain, so it was decided that he should take me to the Civilian Conservation Corps camp up the road and wake up the doctor. This he did with much grumbling about needing his sleep.

Grandfather Curton was a harsh man and told me the consequences of continuing to cry. I was scared. The Camp doctor was awakened. He seemed angry, too. He looked at me and without a word or anything for pain, reached in a drawer, took out what looked like a giant set of pliers, pulled my tooth, and walked back toward his bedroom. There was blood and pain, but I dared not cry. It was a long night which I will always remember.

The experience of that night still influences my view of my maternal Grandfather. Perhaps if adults knew what long memories children had of such events, they would handle the "middle of the night" problems differently. Sometimes I wish I didn't have a good memory of such events, but I do. Most people remember both kindness and the occasional harshness that is experienced, and it just will not fade away.

27 WORDS LEARNED FROM A TRUCKER

My little red wagon and a trucker got me in trouble with my mother. I was playing on the sidewalk near our home at 316 Ziegler Street, Chattanooga, Tennessee, when a farmer in a pickup truck broke down on our street. I was intrigued with the truck and the driver, so I stayed close and watched as he worked on the truck. A wrench slipped, and he hurt his hand and said a few choice words.

Later I turned my wagon over, got a stick, and began to work on the wagon. I didn't know what the words meant, but I thought you had to say them to make the fixing work. So I let out a few choice #%&^*@!*#+ words that Mother overheard. Mother gave me a spanking and asked, "Now, do you know why mama spanked you?" I didn't understand curse words, so I didn't know why she had become so upset. My answer in childish terms went something like this, "Mama, you whipped me, now you don't even know why you did it?"

You guessed it, my smart mouth got me another one, but I still didn't know why. Growing up is sometimes hard to do! I think as an adult, I have also been punished for things I didn't know I did. Life sure gets hard sometimes when one doesn't clearly understand why another person is angry and upset. Sometimes I wish I could remember some of those words the trucker said. They sure would come in handy sometimes; at least, I'd feel good knowing that Mother couldn't hear.

I guess there are good words and bad words. The secret is to know when to and when not to say them. I remember Mother's refrain: "You will give account for every idle word...!" I never did learn what an "idle word" was, but I tried not to say anything that sounded kind of "idle." However, recently when I became upset about something,

I called a friend and shared my feelings, "I don't know all those bad words my mamma beat out of me, would you please "cuss a blue streak" for me? He did - and I felt better.

28   IT RAINED ON MY HAMMOCK

The summer I was nine turned out to be a very bad year. My family usually made a big deal out of an annual fishing and camping trip to Piney Creek. I had heard about this trip many times, but you had to be ten years old to participate. Each person had to carry food, clothing, and camping gear for a week about seven miles across a mountain.

It was a hard trip. It was during WW II, and my Uncle Edward was in from the Navy. He brought a hammock on the camping trip. It sure beat sleeping on the ground. He had to leave two nights early to return to the Navy, so I told him I would carry the hammock out if he would leave it for me to sleep in the rest of the trip. He agreed and left the hammock.

During my first night in the hammock it rained hard, and I deserted the "sleeping under the stars" for the shelter of the rock ledge camp site. The problem was that I was asleep when the rain started and moved to the camp without remembering the process. The next morning I found Cousin Billy Brown sleeping in the hammock; I complained loudly.

I was told what happened and that my cousin Billy had dumped the water out of the hammock the next morning and was just resting until breakfast. Naturally, I didn't believe the story and declared that I would not carry the hammock back, that whoever slept in it could take the hammock back to Uncle Edward's house. I actually believed that they waited until I was asleep and carried me to the camp site just to use the hammock. They protested otherwise. I still do not know the truth of it. All I know is that I didn't sleep in the hammock, and I didn't carry it out of the mountains. Family members still kid me about it raining on my hammock. I guess that's better than raining on my parade.

29   WE ARE THE SHEEP STEALING BUNCH

At a family reunion I couldn't believe that I was kin to all the different folk present. I asked my grandfather about my confusion. He explained that there were several groups of Greens. There was the horse stealing bunch, the sheep stealing bunch, the chicken stealing bunch, the pig stealing bunch, and another bunch that have not been caught yet. I asked to which bunch do we belong? His answer was "The sheep stealing bunch, because we have so many preachers in the family. You see when members move from one church to another, some call this "sheep stealing."

After I was ordained as a minister and assigned a pastorate, I was always aware of this problem when new people joined my church. Normally, I would question their reasons to clarify that they had not been persuaded away from another congregation. I also asked them to get their story straight if someone were to ask why they had changed churches. My hopes were that their explanation would be positive and would include the fact that their new pastor was a "better preacher."

30   I "IS'BUT" HAD THREE PIECES

The family budget almost made us vegetarians. One morning, Mother fried some bacon. It was lean, crisp, and brown. The family ate hardily until the youngest, Wilma Sue, yelled, "All the meat is gone, and I "is'but" had three pieces!"

Meat was not a common item on the Green's breakfast menu, but it was a great addition when mama could afford the price. To complain about having just three pieces speaks to the issue of how "little" small children know about the financial struggles of their parents. This lesson is not learned until one manages a household and feeds their own hungry children. Only then do adults begin to appreciate the struggle it took to bring us through childhood. Raising one's own children is payback time!

31　THE PASTOR ATE MY MEAT

As a growing boy, Mother would attempt to have meat on the menu once a week, usually on Saturday. On one Saturday morning, she cooked cube steak and brown gravy. There was one extra piece which Mother said was mine because I was a growing boy.

During the meal, the pastor dropped in for a brief visit. Out of respect, Mother asked him to eat with us. Normally, I guess this would be an honor, but he took the extra piece of meat, the rest of the good brown gravy, and the last two biscuits. I could hardly listen to that man preach the next Sunday for thinking, "The preacher ate my meat...." It may be hard for some folks, who were not raised poor, to understand what a small piece of meat would mean to a growing boy.

It was certain, my pastor didn't understand. In fact, there are a lot of things pastors don't know. It's wonderful to know the Bible and be educated in theology, but knowing and understanding people is the key to success in the ministry. Someone ought to teach those fellows the practical side...the "rest of the story."

32   TAKE IT WITHOUT MILK

Traveling with some friends to a funeral, we stopped at a small South Carolina town cafe for coffee. One of the crowd ordered "Coffee, without cream." Without hesitation the young waitress responded, "You'll have to take it without milk; we're out of cream." The quick wit of the young waitress provided a comic relief for a group on their way to the funeral of a friend. To be cheerful and witty is always a good thing even if the Coffee Shop is out of cream.

33   WASH AS FAR AS YOU CAN

One summer as a child I visited my Grandmother Curton who had moved to an old hotel on the Hiwassee River near Reliance, Tennessee. I got rather dirty playing outside, and she prepared a #10 wash tub for me to take a bath. She instructed me how to bathe.

"Start with your face and wash down as far as you can. Next, wash your feet and up as far as you can. Then wash your can!" Not a bad set of instructions for a dirty little boy.

34   I'M HUCK FINN'S DADDY

When my youngest son, Brian Lane Green, got his first lead on Broadway, I was excited. It was in "Big River," and he played Huck Finn. During the first few weeks of the show, I had the privilege of going to New York and seeing Brian perform on Broadway. I was so proud.

At Intermission I went to the Men's Room, and two young boys were there washing their hands. I asked, "Do you like the show?" Before they could answer, I blurted out, "I am Huck Finn's father!" One of the boys looked at me and said,

"My daddy's Superman, and his grandfather is John Wayne." I was so proud, I had to tell someone, even if they didn't believe me!

Parents often do not really know their grown children and what they have accomplished. To most of us, our children are still children, then reality hits - you realize that you are older than you want to be. To know that your children have grown into adults and are capable of caring for themselves is a good feeling.

35   BART AND MY MERCEDES

I was proud of my first Mercedes, a 220 Diesel, and that pride caused me to wound my oldest son, Barton. He and his friends were playing basketball on the driveway. A stray ball bounced and broke the Mercedes hood emblem on my new car. I sent Bart to his room and the other boys home. My reaction was harsh, unfair, and wrong. Sometimes it is hard to keep the proper balance between property and people.

Three Mercedes later, Bart asked to borrow my car to drive to North Carolina. His plans were to propose to a beautiful girl, and he wanted to do it in a fancy car. On the way over, during a rain storm, he hydroplaned into a guardrail and destroyed the front end of my beautiful car. He never proposed to the girl. I think he felt that Providence had intervened.

Remembering the basketball episode, my reaction was mature, calm, and fatherly. I have always been glad about the accident; it gave me an opportunity to demonstrate my affection for my son. Hopefully, my response to the incident taught Bart a lesson as well. Was it just a hard rain, or was God demonstrating his love and care for us all, and perhaps giving both of us a second chance? Bart, a chance to rethink his marriage, and me, a second chance to respond, not to a broken emblem on a Mercedes hood, or to the crushed front end of a Mercedes coupe, but to the broken heart of a young man. When I saw the car, the response was "That's the way the Mercedes bends!" I think our father-son relationship was strengthened. It only cost me $500. It was worth every penny. God is good!

36   TOUGH LOVE

Some years ago my niece, Vanessa, came to live with us for a while. She had some difficulties living in California. Notwithstanding her minister father's serving a large Presbyterian church and her mother working as a Psychiatric Nurse, Vanessa's "California" problems persisted. The family thought perhaps Uncle Hollis could make a difference.

I provided Vanessa with some "tough love;" that is, showing affection and adding discipline to the daily routine. Vanessa began to change. A list of rules was structured to bring the needed discipline. Part of this approach was learned from Mother whose work experience included teaching school, raising a family, and serving as Dean of Women at two different educational institutions. Mother had two lists of rules for the women of the college. If certain rules were broken, the individual received a dorm demerit; other infractions produced a school demerit. Actually, it took ten dorm offenses to create a demerit of record for the school. This system worked well for college-aged young women, but would it work for Vanessa?

Vanessa's list of rules had some small insignificant acts or chores and some big no-no's. For example, she had to check the backyard daily to see if the grass was growing. At night, her last chore was to see if the light was out in the fridge. Oh, she also had to listen to at least two of my crazy jokes each day.

It became clear that the routine of doing small things and not breaking small rules was good training for keeping larger commitments. Vanessa grew daily and just before her 18th birthday returned to her parents as a beautiful young lady. Tough love usually works, if the child really feels both loved and responsible. Try it. Children love discipline and the soft "tough love" that points out both parental love and the consequences of breaking rules.

37   MY NUMBERED JOKES

I enjoy telling jokes and funny stories. When my sons, Barton and Brian, and particularly my niece, Vanessa, would say, "I've heard that one!" I would give it a number. Thereafter, when I wanted to tell that particular story or joke, I would simply say 127 or 62. My numbered jokes always got laughs.

Barton, Brian, and Vanessa are grown now, but I still write numbers on their cards or our telephone conversations end with a few numbers. The numbered jokes still bring laughs or at least a smile. I don't know if it is remembering the actually story or joke, or just the pleasure of not having to hear it again. It really doesn't matter, because a laugh, even a smile, is worth a million jokes.

38   KNOWING THE CARS ON SIGHT

Growing up in Chattanooga and visiting my extended family in Rhea County by bus, I learned a simple way to save money. Mother would give me a quarter to ride the bus, but I would hitch-hike and try to stay ahead of the bus. If the bus caught up with me, I would board, but I would save 5 or 10 cents. Sometimes I would make it all the way to the road of my grandparent's house. Along the way I encountered lots of differences between urban and rural living.

One difference, in particular, was the ability to recognize the make, model, and year of most cars that passed, while my country cousins could not. They would see only a few cars each day from a distance, and I was exposed close up to hundreds of cars every day in the city.

My cousin, Donald Pogue, finally figured it all out when he said, "Hollis, you're not smart. You just see more cars than I do!" This was a reality check. It helped me understand that opportunity for learning and willingness to learn are two different things altogether. Later, I learned the difference between "ignorant" meaning "not to know" and "dumb" meaning "cannot learn." My cousins just had not had the city-type opportunity to learn about cars.

One should always take these facts into account when tempted to judge another person or culture as to the level of knowledge on a given subject. I guess Will Roger's idea was correct that "We are all ignorant, just on different subjects." My cousins could do lots of "country" things that were totally foreign to me. Sometimes it made me feel somewhat awkward, but I learned to ask, "Could you teach me how to do that?" A willingness to learn and to permit others to teach creates lasting friendships even between cousins.

39   CANDY STICKS AND ORANGES

My father's oldest brother, William O. Green, (1903-1991), would invite my family to spend the Christmas Holidays with his family. For nine years after the death of my father, we spent the holidays with this loving and happy family. It was William's way to assist a beloved brother's family during the Season when Daddy was missed the most.

Uncle William was poor by some standards, but his family had plenty to eat and there were lots of children with whom to play and plenty of things to do. I learned that family and caring for others makes one rich beyond measure. His wife, Edith Sparks Green, (1910-1991), was a good mother, a great cook, and always managed to make us feel both at home and loved.

One Christmas Eve I shall always remember. Looking out the window, I saw my uncle, who was a big man, carrying on his shoulder a crate and a box of something under his arm. I learned the crate contained oranges, and the box was filled with peppermint stick candy. He had bought it on credit and carried it three miles to make Christmas bright for all the children.

While we sat by the wood fire, Uncle William took out his pocket knife, cut a hole in an orange, stuck a peppermint stick in the hole, and passed it along until everyone had one. Then he showed us how to squeeze the orange and suck the juice through the porous candy stick. It made the juice so sweet and brightened the face of all the children. After all it was Christmas time!

With the fire burning warmly, sweet candy, oranges, and love, we always had a great Christmas. I often sit in the place where his house stood (It is now Green Oak's Park on the campus of Oxford Graduate School) and think of the days of peppermint sticks and oranges. They were the good ole days! I still enjoy peppermint and love to eat oranges because they remind me of my childhood and the Christmas Holidays at Uncle William's house.

40   MY FIRST FISH

The Hiwassee River is often clear and shallow as it flows through Polk County, TN, near Reliance. My maternal Grandfather, Robert Tate Curton, lived near the river in an old hotel. I wanted badly to catch a fish, but I had never been fishing. My father was dead, and I had no big brother to teach me how to fish. There was no one willing to go to the river with me or help me make a fishing pole. I made a big fuss about the whole matter.

Finally, my Aunt Lena Vincent decided to humor me. She bent a straight pin into a crude fish hook and bent the top of the pin over and tied a string about twelve feet long to the pin and attached it to a garden bean pole. She walked over to the river with me and found a safe spot near a shallow place and told me to put the hook in the water and be quiet. To make matters worse, she warned me that I did not have a fishing license, and if the Game Warden caught me fishing I might go to jail. She left with another warning not to go near the water. "You can't catch a fish if they can see you!"

I was as still as a mouse for a long time and nothing happened. I could see fish swimming in the shallow water, but none would take my bait. I decided to put my hook in front of the fish and jerk. This I did several times, but no fish. At last, I was lucky. I snagged a fish in the tail and brought it to the bank. As I landed the fish, I saw a man walking on the railroad bridge that crossed the river. I just knew it was the Game Warden and that my goose was cooked.

I ran across the plowed field dragging the poor fish behind. Aunt Lena was surprised to see me and the fish so she decided to celebrate my first catch. She took water from the rain barrel and put it in a large wash tub and turned my fish loose. It swam vigorously.

The man from the bridge stopped by to chat with Aunt Lena; he wasn't the Game Warden, but I didn't know it. I was scared to death. I just knew he would take me to jail for catching that puny little fish that was not big enough to eat. Aunt Lena put a tablecloth over the tub to hide the fish and said, "Nobody here has been fishing today." He took the cue and made some remarks about the dangers of the river and that only people with a fishing license were allowed to fish. He was just a neighbor, but on a hot summer day he sure stopped my fishing cold. I never did become a good fisherman. I guess I liked catching, but not fishing or cleaning. Oh, I liked eating, too, but not the fishing part. It took too long, and you had to be still and quiet. That was both hard and boring.

I still remember that first fish I snagged in the tail. It was too small to eat. I would not have enjoyed eating it anyway. It would be like trying to eat a trophy you won in some contest. We took it back to the river and turned it loose. It probably grew to be a whopper. I often wonder if anyone ever caught my fish. Every time I see the Hiwassee River, I think and wonder if my fish is still swimming around down there somewhere. Those were the days when aunts and uncles were part of the family and tried to assist the children during their growing up years. I have good memories of my aunts and uncles on both sides of the family. I consider it a thrill to be called "uncle" by a child these days.

41   FUNNY PAPER ON THE WALL

As a child I enjoyed my visits to Aunt Edith's, especially the overnight ones. She managed her house well on a small budget and kept everything clean. One of the ways she kept the walls clean was to paper them with newspaper. It also served as a form of insulation. The bedrooms where the children slept were often papered with the Sunday multiple colored funny papers. I enjoyed reading the comics on the wall and on the ceiling, too.

The site is now called Green Oaks Park. I pass it almost every day, and among other good memories, I think of the funny paper on the wall and Aunt Edith's cooking, especially during the holidays. Her tradition on Easter morning was to have a contest to see which child could eat the most eggs. I never did win, but I enjoyed the eating and the excitement. I always felt full on Easter morning and didn't want to eat eggs for a few days.

42 A 5-DOLLAR BILL UNDER THE LAMP

With my father's death in 1937, three months before he was invested in Social Security, Mother had a tough time raising three children. Mother was an independent woman who would not take charity from anyone. I remember times when Mother prayed for "daily bread" because the groceries would not last until payday. As a growing boy, this was a real concern, but I had confidence in Mother's prayers.

I would rush home from G. Russell Brown Elementary School to see how God had answered Mother's prayer. Sometime I would find groceries. Other times I would find money left, probably by kinfolk. Mother never locked her doors so people could come and go as they pleased. One day I rushed home to find nothing.

Disappointed and discouraged, I wondered what we would do for food. Then my eyes caught a glimpse of something sticking out from under the lamp by my bed in the living room. It was a five (5) dollar bill (lots of money in those days). I knew God had answered Mother's prayer, and we were going to have a feast. Mother took the money to the store and came home to fix the best supper I ever remember eating. I marveled at both Mother's faith and God's marvelous provisions.

I often feel sorry for people who never had to trust God for daily bread. They are truly handicapped in their moral and spiritual development. When material struggles came to my ministry, I would always remember that Mother's God was my God. It gave me courage to push forward. Mother's philosophy was simple, "God knows your deadlines."

43   COLD WATERMELON

One summer when I was young, my grandfather sent me with a mule and harrow to clear out the Lone Mountain peach orchard. It was a big task for a young lad. I carried a large lunch and a watermelon to the orchard. The watermelon was placed in the spring to cool, and I went to work.

Soon I became hot and thirsty and tied up the mule and headed for the spring. I drank lots of water, but was still hot. Watermelon seemed like a good idea. So I ate most of the cool melon. Somehow the cold water, the hot sun, and the cool watermelon didn't jive. I passed out and woke up on my back facing the sun. I was alone. It was scary. I should not have been alone. This is the only time I can remember when my grandfather's judgment was faulty. I guess even grandfathers are human.

An early principle from Genesis speaks about Adam being alone; God said, "It is not good for man to be alone." The wise man Solomon clearly understood the problem of being alone. He said, "Two are better than one; because they have a good reward for their labor. For if they fall, the one will lift up his fellow, but woe to him that is alone when he falleth; for he hath not another to help him up." (Ecclesiastes 4:9-10).

One can learn even from the mistakes of another. My own attitude about young people was shaped by this event. Young people need guidance, boundaries, and love from others around them. It is never good to be alone: companionship and fellowship are important to everyone.

44   A CHERISHED NAVY KNIFE

My sister, Betty, married a Sailor just home from World War II. I was attracted to him at once. He had been in the war and had medals. Without a father or a big brother, George filled a gap in my life. He was good to the family, especially to my mother, and seemed genuinely interested in me. He grew up with brothers and understood that a young boy without a father or brother needed a friend.

One day George gave me the U.S. Navy knife he had carried aboard ship. He had taken heavy string and covered the handle with a special wrapping, covered it with glue, shellac, or something to make it special. This was a special gift, which I guarded with my life. Since I had lost my father's pocket knife I knew the anguish of such loss. For many years the knife reminded me of his role in the family. It became a symbol to me.

After many years of safe keeping, I decided not to pass the Navy knife to one of my own sons, but to return it to George so he could pass it on to a son or grandson. The returning of the knife was a message of great value sent from a brother-in-law to a "big brother." I had kept it safe and returned it in good condition. I had learned a lesson from the loss of my father's pocket knife. I actually don't know who has the knife, but I am sure that the old Navy knife from World War II is a cherished possession for someone close to George D. Stout, Sr.

45   JUST A POUND OF COFFEE

My family moved often with Mother's attempt to find better, more affordable living conditions for her and three children. When my older sister married, her husband (George D. Stout) invited Mother to move in with them.

Mother hesitated and waited to give the newlyweds time to build a life. Early in my sister's marriage, George insisted that Mother and the children move with them to a newly purchased home.

By this time Mother's will had broken down, and she accepted. I was a senior in high school with an after school job in a grocery store. George came to me one day and said, "Your room and board is one pound of coffee each Saturday night." He specified the brand and the grind he wanted. Faithfully, I paid the fare and felt that I was earning my way. It was a nice and good thing for him to do. It taught me that even within a family there must be no "free loading." Each member of a family must carry part of the load and share in family responsibility. It is the fair thing to do! My eternal thanks goes to George for his role in my life and the lives of my family.

46   GRANDFATHER AND THE FAST CAR

One day in a peach orchard my Grandfather Green and I were resting in the shade of a tree as an old car rumbled past. Grandfather said, "See that car? It's probably going 60 miles an hour. That's a mile a minute. When I was a boy, it took papa's yoke of oxen all day to go to town to do trading; now they go there, buy something, and are back in fifteen minutes." While I was trying to grasp "a mile a minute," he continued, "The world is getting so fast, I'm afraid it's going to fall apart!" Now I was concerned . . . a mile a minute . . . the world's going to fall apart before I grow up. I felt like saying, "Stop the world, I want to get off!"

I decided I had better grow up fast or I might miss the whole thing. I had a different perspective on the world after that lesson in speed. I've been in a hurry ever since.

I am kind of like the old Indian who had been running for a long time and stopped suddenly. Others thought it was to rest, but the tough old Indian said it was to let "his spirit catch up with his body."

Therefore, I occasionally rest just to let my "spirit" catch up with me. Who would want to go forward without his spirit? Maybe it would be good for all of us to slow down and smell the roses, watch the birds, and let our spirits catch up. Flowers and birds speak to the care of a loving Heavenly Father and make us aware that a Mighty Force is watching over the World and all the creatures great and small. This includes me and you!

47   A PEACH TOO FAR

Peach picking time on Lone Mountain was always a ticklish subject. Peach fuzz got everywhere, and it could itch something awful. This year there were lots of peaches, and my grandfather had a little contest going to see who picked the most. I was picking from a ladder and needed one more good peach to complete my basket. I extended my reach a little too far and down came ladder, basket, peaches, and me.

While picking up the peaches from the ground, I thought about what I had done. It would have been easier and quicker to climb down and move the ladder. I just needed one more peach. Why couldn't I reach just one more? My arms have always been short, but I only needed one more peach. It was difficult to admit that it wasn't just an accident. I had actually caused the fall and knocked myself out of the prize. I don't remember what the prize was. All I remember was that I did not win it. It was probably a beautiful, ripe peach, just like the one I was reaching for when I fell. Well, I guess one can't have everything: good looks, health, the best family in the world, great cousins, good uncles and aunts, and just one more peach to fill my basket. I still remember that summer, the ladder and a peach too far! In fact, I now live just steps away from where this actually happened. I pass the spot every day. What is the lesson? Ambition and energy must be balanced with wisdom and care. I learned that over reaching had consequences. Now, that's a good lesson.

48   THREE PEAS IN A POD

My younger sister's grandsons, Kyle and Joel, were visiting. They were into everything. Even though they had a toy drawer at our house, they constantly wanted something else. They wanted to go outside, inside, to town, to the park, to the lake, anywhere but where they were. In exasperation, my wife came up with one of her famous Gail-isms: "Those two are three peas in a pod if there ever was one." These are not the only Gail-isms. Someday I may write a whole book full of her witty sayings. For example:

"I'm just not going to talk with you until we learn to communicate!"

"Don't feel bad because you don't feel good."

"God has been dealing with me about talking too spiritual." Etc., etc., etc...!

49   WE DON'T HAVE A BIG DRIPPER

When my sister's grandsons moved to Charlotte, North Carolina, they were greatly missed. My wife had spent many hours with them. One of her favorite things to do in the evening when they were visiting was to make a pallet in the backyard and teach the children about the constellations. We live in a small rural community, and there are no bright lights to hinder the viewing of the sky at night. The boys especially enjoyed finding the Big Dipper. A few days after they moved to the big city, Gail got a call. One of the boys said, "Aunt Gail, we can't see the big drip-per!" The bright lights of a big city had made it difficult for them to see the constellations. This made me aware that children need more than just a few nights of viewing the stars to learn about Astronomy so I am writing a children's book, The Shimonaka Big Drip-per, and including a brief course on Astronomy for children. You may purchase this book and other good books at [www.gea-books.com]. Oh, you are wondering how "Shimonaka" got in the title: their father had Japanese ancestors.

50   FARMER JOHN CHEESE

My wife enjoys fixing spaghetti, especially when the boys are visiting. One evening as we were about to begin eating, Gail asked the older boy, Kyle, "Do you want some Parmesan Cheese on your spaghetti?" Joel, the little one, piped up, "I want some Farmer John cheese, too!" You guessed it; that's what Parmesan Cheese has been called at our house from that day forward. Since the ketchup people are now selling ketchup in various colors to attract children, "Farmer John Cheese" could be a marketing concept for a children's package of Parmesan Cheese. Perhaps Joel could get royalty.

51   NIGHT RIDE ON A MOTOR SCOOTER

When I was a senior in high school, Donald Aultman was the minister of music at my church. Donald was single, and on Sunday evenings after church, we would ride his motor scooter across town to Highland Park Baptist to attend a radio broadcast. "The Back Home Hour" followed the regular service and had both music and preaching. Three beautiful sisters sang a trio on the broadcast almost every Sunday night. Sibling harmony is the best, and when that harmony is accompanied by female beauty, it makes a young man want to go to church.

One night it was announced that one of the trio was getting married. Donald and I began to lose some spiritual fervor for attending the late night service. It just wasn't the same after we knew she was "spoken for" and would soon be "somebody's wife."

A few years ago I met Dr. Lee Robinson in the Atlanta Airport. He had been retired for many years, but we chatted about the days of the Sunday night broadcast and the beautiful ladies that sang. When I told him that Donald and I lost interest after the wedding, he responded that there was a noticeable drop in attendance about that time. The ebb and flow that draw young men to church are often obscure, but sometimes it's as obvious as a beautiful girl. Come to think of it, church is where I found my wife.

52   NOODLE POP, THE PIG

When my youngest sister, Sue, was a small child, she encountered an albino piglet. My Aunt Margie Vineyard had separated it from the litter for a pet. Aunt Margie named the piglet, "Noodle Pop." Aside from the small white pig running loose, my sister thought all the pigs were noodle pops. For several years all pigs were called by that endearing name.

One day Noodle Pop was gone - not just gone, but he had been sent to the market. I don't know when, or if ever, Sue got over her reluctance to eat pork. She thought she might be eating little "Noodle Pop." Pets can be endearing to a child, and the loss of a pet is a real blow to the little understood dynamics of separation. Childhood pets are a good way to learn about separation and even death so the big surprises of life are not so traumatic. Perhaps we should be sure each child experiences the love of a pet.

53   THE HILL BRAKE AND A FRIEND

Since my father's death (October 8, 1937), we had not owned a car. I learned to drive on my uncle's farm tractor. At age 10, I could shift the gears, steer, brake, and do various farm jobs that required the driving of a tractor. When I turned sixteen, the music director of my church (Roosevelt Miller) asked my mother if he could take me to get my driver's license. Of course, Mother agreed and thanked him for his interest in me.

Roosevelt owned a funny looking Studebaker. He gave me a Drivers Book to study and took me for a test drive. Stopping on a hill, he shared that the driving test would probably require me to stop and start on a hill. He explained about not letting the car roll backward. Building my confidence, he said, "Put the car in first gear and see if you can get started on this hill without rolling backward more than a few inches." I did it without rolling back an inch. He commended me and said the police would be impressed. My confidence soared.

With confidence I took the driver's test and passed the hill test with commendation from the police. It was months later that I learned about the hill brake on Studebaker cars that prevented them from rolling backward when one pushed in the clutch. I have always wondered, "Did the policeman know about the Studebaker's hill brake?" Perhaps it was the confidence gained from Roosevelt's encouragement? I hardly ever stop on a hill that I don't remember his kindness.

Recently, at the funeral of a mutual friend, I saw his widow and shared my memories about the Studebaker. She remembered the car, but didn't know that many years before

her husband had befriended a fatherless boy and helped
him become a confident man. Good memories are as good as
medicine. Friends are better than money in the bank; you can
access the interest without diminishing the worth and value of
the friendship.

54   CRAMMING FOR THE FINAL

One day my Grandmother, Mattie Barton Green, (1883-
1966), sat on the front porch rocking and reading the big
family Bible. One of her grandchildren asked her what she
was doing. Grandmother responded, "Cramming for my final
exams." Seeing Grandmother meditate and read the Bible
was always a source of comfort for me. Grandparents have
much more influence on their grandchildren than they ever
realize. The influence works even after they are gone.
Hardly a day passes that I don't remember something they
said and did, especially the attention they gave me and their
interest in my life and career.

55   PLOWING A STRAIGHT LINE

My Grandfather Green could plow a straight furrow. One
day I asked him to teach me. He turned me loose with a
mule and a plow. The furrow looked as if a drunken cowboy
had just staggered back to the ranch. Grandfather took the
plow and cut a straight line that would have been the envy of
any surveyor. Having discovered that I could not learn on my
own, I was ready to learn the lesson of the straight furrow.

Grandfather reminded me of the barrel of a rifle which
had a near and a far sight. He told me to pick out a near
object, such as a fence post, and a distant object, perhaps
a tree, and to align them the same way I would the sights
of a rifle. Doing so, I plowed to the other end of the field.

Looking back, I was surprised at the straight line. I had learned a good lesson.

Grandfather explained that by keeping the near goal in line with the distant goal, the straight line was possible. Since the shortest distance between two points is a straight line, I learned that keeping short range goals and long range goals in perspective saves time and makes things look good, too.

56   YELLOW APPLES ON A RED APPLE TREE

In my Grandfather Green's front yard was a small red apple tree, but one of the branches produced an apple yellowish in color. I was curious, so he explained that the branch producing the yellow apple was grafted into the red apple tree. I was fascinated. How do you do that? How does it work?

With great patience Grandfather explained the process of splitting the branches in a specific way and placing them together. He then showed me about binding them together tightly with twine and covering the whole joint area with bee's wax. He shared that the grafting process was limited because the new branch was a "taker" and not a "giver." Nature nourishes trees with a supply of a watery liquid called sap. It moves upward in part through an intricate supply system. It seems for the most part the grafted branch sucks nourishment from the roots of the host tree, but it doesn't give anything back. Other branches assist the tree through sap-lifting forces created by evaporation and transpiration. This is a kind of breathing water through the leaves. The grafted branch doesn't do this.

The grafted branch uses all the sunshine and rain on its leaves to produce its own yellow apple. It is a strain on the original tree, because the grafted branch actually takes sap away from the other branches bearing red apples. Too many grafts and they would suck the life out of a tree in the process of producing apples.

I learned a lesson about givers and takers and realized that most of us at sometime or the other may be on both ends of that stick. Takers should work at giving, and givers should not begrudge their giving. Scripture is clear, "It is more blessed to give than to receive." I understood that a life of ministry was one of giving not taking.

This philosophy has permeated my adult life and assisted my knowledge of church growth, evangelism, and the development of educational institutions. An understanding of the concept of grafting may clarify the problem as it relates to the integration of communities. One does not have to be a horticulturist to see the disadvantage of foliage without fruit or different kinds of fruit growing on the same tree. Such groups become "takers" without giving a fair share commitment to the infrastructure, which forms the basis for their existence. It's kind of like extended dependence on government; one receives but does not return in taxes.

Scripture in Romans 11 explains a conceited and egotistical perspective, which resulted in "taking without giving." The character of a grafted branch illustrated the idea. Paul said, "You do not support the root, but the root supports you." A grafted branch does not support the root, which nourishes its life, but the root supports the engrafted branch. The grafted branch may live, grow, produce foliage and even fruit, but remains an unorthodox part of the larger unit. It often becomes militant and radical and is a liability to the original unit. The graft may also become a hindrance to growth and fruit bearing by sapping strength from the source. This may explain the advance of denominations at the expense of Christianity.

My firm belief is that social integration and church growth would be much easier if everyone understood the problems of grafting. An individual or a group cannot long take from the nourishing roots of Governments or Christianity without giving back their unreserved loyalty and support for the cause of unity in both government and religious life. I wrote four books about this whole subject, <u>Discipleship</u>, <u>Why Churches Die</u>, <u>Why Christianity Fails in America</u>, and <u>Titanic Lessons</u>. These books may be purchased from the website at www.gea-books.com. Click on Books A to Z.

57   RIDING THE COUPLING POLE

My Grandfather Green gave me a job during hay cutting time. The barn was on a hill, and I was supposed to run along behind the wagon, loaded with hay, and scotch the wheels when the mules needed a rest. I placed several large stones up the hill to the barn. After several loads of hay and several scotching episodes, I became tired.

Seeing the coupling pole sticking out behind the wagon, I decided to straddle it and ride awhile. Forgetting myself, the mules got tired, stopped, and the wagon began to roll back. Finally, with Grandfather's commands the mules were able to stop the backward movement of the wagon with a jerk. With the jolt, the hay slid off the back of the wagon and carried me off the coupling pole.

When Grandfather dug me out from under the hay, he reminded me, "You can't just ride the coupling pole, son, you must scotch the wagon!" The understood lesson was clear: one can't just take a free ride without understanding the responsibilities to the tasks at hand. When one fails to do assigned tasks, it makes more work for everyone. And sometimes it creates circumstances that produce serious accidents.

I never forgot my coupling pole ride, my "fall from grace," or the feeling at the bottom of a load of hay on a rocky hill road, with the sound of a wagon, two mules, and Grandfather above. When you know it is your fault, the lesson is a hard one to learn. Such lessons stick with you all your days, nights, and weekends. The worst part of the error of my ways was that I disappointed my grandfather who always expressed such confidence in me and my ability to accomplish great things. I have worked hard all my life to compensate for such failures in my youth.

58   TOBACCO JUICE ON A BEE STING

My mother taught me that tobacco was bad. This was when tobacco was socially acceptable and widely used. Mother insisted that it was a nasty habit and bad for one's health. One day visiting my grandfather's farm, I was stung by a honeybee. Grandfather made a poultice with tobacco juice and something and placed it on my wound. I protested that tobacco was bad stuff and that Mother would not like it.

Grandfather explained that "Poison kills poison." Since the bee sting was poison, this "bad stuff" that your mother doesn't like could cure it. He went on to explain the medicinal values of various herbs and potions. Later I learned that my grandfather was not only a farmer, he was a good herbalist.

His brother was a Medical Doctor (William Thomas Green, M.D. 1857-1939), and doctored with regular prescription medicine those who could pay. Grandfather Green had read all his brother's medical books, but couldn't prescribe medicine, so he used herbs and natural things to doctor the poor folks and the animals. Grandfather was known among the community as Doc Green; in fact, that is what is on his tombstone. Grandfather didn't get to go to medical school, but he learned a lot about medicine and used it to help

others. Sometimes one does learn good lessons from bad
things.

Since Grandfather didn't charge for his services some
people took advantage of his kindness. On one occasion
a man returned several times for free advice and finally
asked if Grandfather could cure his bald spot. With great
enthusiasm Grandfather answered in the affirmative. He
wrote a prescription and solicited the man's assistance.

Prescription: 2 ounces of Diospyrous (green persimmon)
juice; 2 tablespoons of Gallus domesicus (domestic chicken)
manure mixed with Carbonaes or medical petroleum jelly.
Apply 3X per day for 2 wks. --ALP Green

The man wanted the remedy immediately so Grandfather
sent him to the chicken house with a tea cup and asked
him to get 2 tablespoons of fresh chicken manure. Then
he sent him to a persimmon tree for 2 green persimmons.
Grandfather then mashed the green persimmons for the juice
and mixed it with the chicken manure; he then added a little
carbonated Vaseline and put it in a salve tin with instructions.
Rub this on your bald spot three times a day for two weeks.
The natural question was "How does it work?"

Grandfather's answer: "The green persimmon juice will
shrink the bald spot, the chicken manure will color the spot,
and the odor will keep people at a distance; it will then look
like you have more hair."

I understand that this "free-loader" never returned
for more medical attention. But I had lots of confidence
in Grandfather's knowledge and as I got older and began
losing my hair, I considered using his hair loss remedy. The
problem: I lived in the city and fresh chicken manure was
hard to find. There were no green persimmons either. It
probably wouldn't have worked anyway since hair loss is
probably hereditary. I do remember the advice of an elderly

woman when I began my hair loss: "Be careful young man, you're getting room for another face. Don't become "two-faced" or people won't like you!"

59   NAME IN GRANDFATHER'S BIBLE

My Grandfather Green had the custom of reading several chapters in the Bible each day. As he read, he would write in the margin the names of the people who came by his place during the day. In his evening prayers, he would pray for the people whose names appeared in the margin of the passages he had read that day. It was a great joy to discover my name in the margin of Grandfather's Bible and to know he had prayed for me many times.

Grandfather's effort to teach me the lessons of life after my father died became a central part of who I am today. God give us more good parents and grandparents! They are desperately needed to keep the next generation on the straight and narrow way. I personally discovered it was difficult to be too broad minded and walk the narrow way that leads to life eternal. After all, it is the eternal things that really count, now and forever. Grandfather's prayers joined with Mother's prayers became a fence on both sides of the road that kept me on the straight path. Thanks to all for a good life.

60   DEER ANTLERS ON THE PORCH

My paternal Grandfather was most attentive to me after the death of my father, his son. He took pains to teach me to fire a rifle, catch a fish, trap a rabbit, plow a mule, repair tack for the animals, care for the dogs, function in a remote campsite, work a crop, and live together in harmony with all associates regardless of race, creed, color, or origin.

Grandfather taught me the difference between social integration and family relations. He made me aware of my English heritage and the family's loyalty to the King during the Revolution and to the Union during the Civil War. He taught me about grafting trees and preparing for the next day's work, but most of all he provided me a spiritual example of commitment to family, church, and country.

One day I asked him about the deer antlers hanging over his front door. He told me the story of a 1901 "punkin ball" shot with an old Daniel Boone type rifle from many yards away. He showed me the place on Lone Mountain he stood and where the deer was standing. It was the last deer he ever shot. After the story, I asked if I could have the antlers when I grew up. He said they were mine, but that they should hang over his door until his death. Those antlers hang in my home office today and are a constant reminder of "Granddaddy Green." Here is how the antlers finally arrived in my possession.

Grandfather had a strong sense of Providence and thought he would know when his "time came to die." He would say, "My little dogs know when they are going to die and go off into a secluded place. Surely if a dog knows, I will know." At times when he was ill he would refuse to call the children in because, "It is not my time." On one occasion the hospital had given him 17 units of blood, and it looked as if it would be the end. He told the young doctor, "You are going to let me die from internal bleeding, and it is not my time."

Grandfather asked a daughter to go home to his medicine chest (he was a good herbalist) and make some tea from several specified ingredients. She did, and he drank it. The internal bleeding stopped, and he lived many more years. On December 26, 1963, he asked the doctors to call in his children. The custom was to go in to see their father in the order of their birth, oldest to the youngest. My father was the third child. He asked that I come in my father's place.

When I entered the room that Thursday, December 26, 1963, he greeted me warmly and asked if I were scheduled to preach in my church on Sunday. My answer was affirmative. He told me to drive to my church in South Florida and preach on schedule. He said that nothing was more important than fulfilling my ministry responsibility. He knew that by the time I arrived in South Florida he would be dead (December 27, 1963), and I would be unable to drive back in time for his funeral. This was his strategy to protect me. He told one of his daughters, "Hollis lost one father. I sent him home so he would not be here when I die, but list him as the officiating minister at my funeral even though he can't make it to the service."

Then on his death bed he remembered the promise of the deer antlers. He sent one of my uncles with instructions to take down the antlers and save them for me. Each time I notice the antlers, I am reminded of his special concern for me. I never saw an obituary of my grandfather until over 30 years later. When my Aunt Marie Pogue Truex gave me a box of pictures, I found an obituary and was surprised to see my name listed as the officiating minister. When I questioned it, I was told about Granddaddy's death bed conversation regarding the antlers and his respect for my ministry. Even from the grave, Grandfather reminded me of his affection and concern for me and of the importance of life's commitments and one's responsibility to serve others.

61   YOU'RE GOING TO DIE ANYWAY

Mother was getting old, and my sister in California kept saying to her family, "I want to move back to Tennessee before Mother dies." Some years passed, grandchildren were born to my sister, and they received the same message that Nanna Green was getting old and was going to die, so they better hurry and move back to Tennessee.

Finally, the day came when they all moved back and came to visit Mother. Living alone with no small children around, Mother's apartment was filled with little knick knacks setting all around. When the two young great-grandsons began to mess with Mother's "stuff," she cautioned them not to break anything. Then one of the boys said, "Oh, it's alright, you're going to die anyway!" As the family recovered, another found Mother's pantry. It was a large closet filled with shelves of canned goods that Mother kept stocked in case she couldn't go to the store. The great-grandson asked, "Nanna Green, when you die, can I have your store?"

Death is an evident part of life. It would be great if adults could view death in such a matter of fact way as children do. To be religious about death one should remember that Scripture tells us to weep when a child is born (anticipating life's troubles) and rejoice when death, (the final victory), the ultimate healing, the door to Eternity is reached. "Precious in the sight of the Lord is the death of His saints!"

I guess the key is to become a "saint," but what is a saint? I asked a young boy this question, and his answer was, "A Saint is someone the light shines through." What he knew about saints was from stained-glass windows in church. Each Sunday morning the sun would shine through the pictures of Saints in the stained-glass. Not a bad definition and a rather good understanding. Does God's light shine through you? Do little children see the "goodness of a saint" in you? When God's Light shines through you to a child, that child sees a Saint!

62   PROFIT AT THE FARMER'S MARKET

Mother was a widow with three children. She gave up her teaching job because she couldn't provide for her family during the summer. She took a job in a textile mill making $6 to $8 a week. I was the middle child with two sisters. I began working at age 10, doing what I could to help. By the time I was fourteen, an uncle, (Robert Hiram Green), was letting me work during the summer of 1947 at the Farmer's Market in Chattanooga selling his farm produce. Hiram would continually restock with fresh products. This required me to stay overnight and sleep in the truck. My uncle would let me eat out of the money I collected, and I enjoyed the freedom, trust, and a taste of independence.

Realizing that many of the farmers wanted to go home at night, I would patrol the market about closing time looking for farmers with unsold produce who didn't want to stay overnight. Since I had to stay overnight anyway, I would use my uncle's money and buy their produce at a bargain so they could go home. The next morning I would sell the extra produce at a profit. I would put my uncle's money back and pocket the profit. Some weeks I would make more money than my mother in this way.

It was a time of growing and understanding how things worked. At the end of the summer, my uncle would give me a small stipend, reminding me he had fed me all summer, and I would thank him. It was years before he knew that I had used his money to make a profit for myself. Naturally, Mother thought my uncle had paid me well. The lesson learned was that one must take advantage of every good opportunity to work hard and earn an honest dollar. The money was a great boost to the family income and provided for my clothes and spending money for school.

Later I learned that most businessmen use the bank's money to front their products, then they use their profit to pay back the loan with interest. It seems I had a better deal; I used Hiram's money without paying interest. Everybody won: Hiram got a worker to stay at the Farmer's Market and sell his produce, and I made an extra profit from buying and selling. It was a time of learning; the money was a help, too.

63   I DIDN'T HAVE AN EXPERIENCE BASE

Growing up I was somewhat sheltered. Mother protected me from myself and others who would lead me down the wrong path. When I heard preachers give witness to things that had happened in their lives, I realized that as a young man I did not have an experience base from which to work. I needed some "stories" to share.

While still a senior in high school an opportunity came to witness a young man (Clyde Still) die in the Tennessee Electric Chair, and I accepted the challenge. I traveled to Nashville with a group of clergy and was introduced to the young black man who was going to die. Talking with him for a while, he opened up and shared his story. Clyde was in the wrong place, with the wrong people, at the wrong time. Hitchhiking, he was picked up by two men who decided to pick up a young white girl and rape her. He fled in fear for his life losing his wallet on the back seat. They raped her and in the process killed the girl. The Brother told me he had nothing to do with the rape or the killing, but there was no one alive to clear him. One of the rapists was killed while being captured. The other one was shot while trying to escape. He alone was left to pay for their crime of rape and murder.

Clyde Still was married. His wife sang in a gospel quartet with Clevant Derricks, the man who wrote "When God Dips His Pen of Love in My Heart." His family came to visit on Death Row that last night. The undertaker who was to take his body back home stopped by to say a word. I was getting some good stuff to share, but the actual execution made a mark on my life. Race was involved. The Brother claimed to be innocent. The last thing he said to me was clearly a message to young people, "Tell them to watch their company and not take chances. I've done some bad things in my short life, but God has forgiven me for each and every one. I am going to die for something that I did not do." I never believed a man would lie, just thirteen steps from the Electric Chair.

For years when I heard a "certain noise" or the sound of an electrical short, I would panic. Even recently, Gail decided to stop using the automatic end-of-cycle buzzer on the clothes dryer because she noticed that I jumped at the loud sound. Through the years, I have attempted to share the Brother's story with hundreds of teenagers. Someday, I will tell him about my journey and how his life and death affected me and those who heard his story. At seventeen, I was the youngest person ever to witness an execution in Tennessee.

I believed Clyde Still to be innocent, and his death made an impact on my young life. For this reason I have always asked to be off the jury for a capital crime. As long as the system permits the rich to go free and the poor to languish on death row, my thesis will be: it is better to let guilty men go free than to execute one innocent one. I am certain there are crimes for which the guilty should pay the ultimate penalty; however, I shall personally leave that judgment to a higher power.

64   DO THIS WHILE YOU ARE RESTING

My grandfather got up early and began his work on the farm. During the heat of the day he would return for lunch and rest in the shade of the porch or the big apple tree. While he rested he would file his saw, sharpen various tools, or mend harnesses. If I were working with him in the field, he would say after lunch time, "Here son, do this while you are resting." He knew the body needed rest after a meal, but it wasn't a strain on the body to do a few light chores while resting in the shade. This was a good work ethic and I have tried to "stay busy" all my life doing "stuff" even when I was resting.

It has not yet come clear to me how to work while you asleep, but if grandfather were still alive, he probably would find a way to use some newfangled gadget to get things done while he slept. That seems to be the next logical step in relation to his work ethic. He often said things such as, "An idle mind is the devil's workshop and busy hands keep the mind working and that keeps the devil away." Now, if I sense the devil is close by I start working with my hands. It works, kind of like snapping your fingers keeps elephants away.

SECTION TWO
Courtship, Marriage, and Relatives

65   MARRYING SAM'LL DO IT

During the war years many servicemen were married on short furloughs. Staying overnight one Saturday in the home of a clergyman, the doorbell rang about 11:00 PM. A sailor at the door told the preacher he was on leave and about to be shipped overseas and wanted to get married. "I finally talked her into it and am afraid to wait until tomorrow. Would you marry us now?"

Willing to oblige the eager young man, the sailor turned and whistled to the girl waiting in the car and yelled, "Marrying Sam'll do it! Come on in!" My clergy friend hastily put on his marrying suit and shoes, his wife played the wedding music, and the embarrassed bride-to-be came in dressed in a skirt and sweater. In a few minutes they were joined together forever and rushed off to celebrate the few hours left of his leave. I marveled at how a few minutes could change two people's lives forever.

Marriage has a certain risk since about one-half of all marriages in the USA fail. At times this brief ceremony is for better; at other times, it is for worse. Notwithstanding, the vow of faithfulness till death is often the demise of the relationship in advance of the physical death of the parties involved. Why is it so hard to keep the early excitement alive in a relationship? I have finally finished a book started many years ago, How to Build a Better Spouse Trap—How to Stay Married by Really Trying. (www.gea-books.com) I wonder what happened to the young soldier and his bride. Did he make it home from the war? Did their marriage survive the separation?

66 MARRIAGE IS NOT MULTIPLE CHOICE

Weddings are trying times for pastors: so many things
to do with so many telling others how to do them. At a
wedding rehearsal with Jerry and Carolyn Bare, I was going
over the parts that the bride and groom were to repeat. I
read, "Do you take this woman whose hand you hold to be
your lawful wedded wife, for better or worse; for richer or
poorer; in sickness and in health..." As it was repeated, the
groom selected better, richer, health... Trying to keep a
straight face, I stopped and reminded him that the marriage
ceremony was not multiple choice. It was all or nothing.
You can't have the milk unless you buy the whole cow. The
groom's response was, "You can't fault a man for trying."

Many seek shortcuts in relationships; it is also clear that
these shortcuts short circuit the peace and tranquility of
home and hearth. Could this be the real problem in modern
family life? If so, we should encourage everyone to accept
and fulfill all obligations and responsibilities related to society
and in particular to family life.

67 DO YOU HAVE A HUSBAND?

Seeing a young lady in church without a man for several
weeks, I became interested. Observing her devotion, her
interest in music, her involvement with children, and her
general demeanor, my heart spoke to me. When one's heart
speaks, it has a compelling voice and demands action. The
church was near Dobbins Air Force Base, and I thought
perhaps her husband was in the Air Force on TDY assignment
somewhere. Planning to leave the area for a while, I decided
I must find out whether or not she was married. I went up
to her and asked,

"Do you have a husband?"

She answered simply, "No."

"Do you want one?" I asked cautiously.

"Yes." was her unequivocal answer.

"Could we talk about it?"

She agreed, and a few months later (February 8, 1974) we were married. That began a beautiful friendship; it grew into a sweet companionship, and developed into a spiritual fellowship. God is good!

68　ONE LITTLE WORD

I was reluctant to marry again, not wanting to give up my newly discovered independence. After the "Do you have a husband?" episode, I waited two weeks and called her. It was Halloween. We arranged to meet for brunch the next day since I was leaving town for several weeks. She told me she couldn't talk because her parents were visiting. I didn't understand, but gave her my telephone number and told her to call when she had time to talk. Her mother asked, "Who was that on the phone?" When Gail responded, "Dr. Hollis Green," her mother retorted, "Why is he calling you?"

At this her father, the Reverend Henry M. Parks, spoke up and said, "If Dr. Green is calling Gail, it's O.K.; I know him through his books, and he is a good man." Gail called, and we met mid-morning for brunch. The rest is history!

When I returned from my trip, my heart was pounding with anticipation, but nothing prepared me for one little "word" she spoke. During the conversation she said, "When we get married, I'll be good to you. When we get married, my love will always be true." That one word, "when," has been a key to my happiness these many years.

Just to remember, with thanksgiving, that Providence brought us together, is to create a cohesiveness that enhances our time together. How could one word, and one person, make such a difference in the life of a man? That is one of the great mysteries of life! I learned that marriage could work if both work at it every day.

69 LOVE AND COURTSHIP

During my brief courtship with Gail, I sent her a small greeting booklet which she kept through the years. Inside the cover, I wrote my understanding of L O V E in an acrostic:

LOVE IS:

L-earning from the past;

O-pening your heart to someone;

V-iewing the future with confidence;

E-njoying the present moment.

Through the years we have referred to this acrostic many times to "improve our communications." The booklet was placed in the tower "Quiet Time Room" at Oxford Chapel. Hopefully, it will assist others.

70 COMMUNICATION PROBLEMS

Early in my marriage, Gail and I were having trouble communicating about important things. One day, in the heat of "a failure at communication," she said, "I'm just not going to talk with you until we learn to communicate!" We learned, and life gets better day by day and year by year.

The family motto now is "Come and walk along with me, the best is yet to be!" We enjoy the present moment and try to fix things as they "come loose." I learned part of this technique from my Uncle William.

On one occasion William and Edith had a slight disagreement about something. He went outside and sat backward in a straight chair under a tree. As the sun began to go down behind Lone Mountain, he called to the house and said, "Edith, it's getting dark!" She ignored him. He called again, but no response from his wife. Evidently they had agreed to make things right between them, according to scripture, "before the sun goes down."

I was a small child and didn't understand exactly what was happening, and asked their son, Paul, "What's this all about?" His response, "Mom and dad had a little disagreement, and she is teaching him a lesson." The part about "Don't let the sun go down on your wrath" stuck with me through the years. It has certainly lessened the "lack of communication" between Gail and me. We have two plaques hanging in the entry hall of our home. One was purchased when we were first married and reads, "Love spoken here!" The other plaque was written by Jewish Rabbi Ben Ezra and reads:

> Grow old along with me. The best is yet to be.
> The last of life for which the first was made,
> Our times are in His hands.

71   GAILISMS

My wife, Gail, has an unusual way of saying things. My son, Bart, keeps a list of them and refers to her unique statements as "Gailisms". The list started with an early problem in our relationship when we were having difficulty communicating. Through the years she has added more Gailisms to the list.

On one occasion when our two grand nephews Kyle and Joel visited us, Gail said, "Those two are three peas in a pod if there ever was one!" Another day when Vanessa was feeling down, she said, "Don't feel bad because you don't feel good."

One morning during coffee, she shared a "spiritual insight" with me. She said, "God has been dealing with me about talking too spiritual." Then, just the other day, I took her to a special little Tea House for lunch. Her comment, "This sure was an unexpected surprise." Immediately after lunch, I e-mailed Bart; here is another one for your "Gailism File." The best one is still "I'm just not going to talk to you until we learn to communicate."

72   PHONE BOOK IN THE MICROWAVE

My son, Barton, was at the house and wanted to make a phone call, but could not find the telephone book. He looked high and low. Finally, he called to Gail and asked, "Where is the phone book?" "In the microwave," was the reply. Neither he nor I could believe our ears. He found it, used it, and put it back in the microwave. Later that evening he opened the microwave in preparation to warm something and called out, "Why is the phone book in the microwave?" Gail responded, "I put it there so I could find it!"

73   ARE YOU A DEMOCRAT?

Soon after our marriage, I took Gail to visit my Aunt Lena Vincent. Her daughter, Irene, better known as "Skeet" was introduced. As she peered directly into Gail's eyes, Irene abruptly asked, "Are you a Democrat?" Fortunately, the answer was "No." In defense of the question, one would have to understand the lack of social skills that precipitated the question. No one knows what would have happened if Gail had been a Democrat.

Notwithstanding this, there was a deeper reason for the question. My family has been Republicans for many years. My father was head of the Young Republicans in Tennessee during the Great Depression. It was a matter of principle. Family unity was at stake. So, to Skeet, it was important that I not bring some liberal Democrat into the family.

Some in Gail's famiy were staunch Democrats; could it be that she is a "democrat mole" trying to find out the Green family political secrets? During the Reagan years, I was confident of her loyalty, but since my friend, George H.W. Bush, lost to Bill Clinton and Bob Dole couldn't unseat him, I am just not altogether sure.

With all the powder, paint, lotions, dress designers, and political spin including all the smoke and mirrors, one can't always tell a book by the cover. Hopefully, by the year 2012, I'll know for sure. Until then I have cautioned the family not to "talk politics" around Gail. It's better to be safe than sorry.

74   HOLLIS IS OK

When I became seriously involved with Gail, she invited me to visit her family in Knoxville. Her Brother Henry was a "mess" and always played pranks on Gail's boyfriends.

When Henry heard that Gail was bringing a preacher boyfriend to meet the family, he told some of the family that Gail didn't need an old "stick in the mud" preacher for a husband and that he was going to play a joke on him.

When we arrived, Henry came to me and said, "We have a family orgy every Friday night. I just wanted you to be aware so you wouldn't be embarrassed." I asked, "What time does it start, and can I bring a friend?" He told Gail, "Hollis is O.K." With his blessing and the family's acceptance we were soon married.

75 I "NOT" YOUR FRIEND

Marrying into a large family, I began to court the small children by claiming to be their "friend." The youngest (Jason Sise) came up to me and clearly said, "I not your friend!" Cultivated over the years, he is now grown, married, and has a son of his own. He was proud to show his friend, "Uncle Hollis," his new son (Connor MacKenzie Sise, born November 14, 1997).

Children learn quickly and identify with those who show them affection. Children are God's gifts to both families and the world at large. We must befriend them and cause them to feel loved. The scripture is clear: "He that hath friends must first show himself friendly." One must never be turned back by the shyness of a child. Friendship requires mutual trust and affection. When big hands reach out; little hands will reach back. To make a child your friend is to make the world a better place.

76 MOTHER WAS BORN TO HARD TIMES

My mother, Grace Curton Green, (1905-1996), was born to hard times and experienced World War I, the Great Depression, the death of a young husband at age 31, experienced World War II, and raised and educated three children as a single parent. When my father died in 1937, he was not yet invested in Social Security. It was natural that she would develop a harsh and negative view of life. One day Mother and I were drinking coffee in a small shop, and she commented, "This is the worst coffee I have ever had!" The comment was made loud enough for most in the small shop to hear.

I was struggling to begin a new graduate school and trying to remain positive in my general attitude. It was difficult, during those days, to be around Mother without some "negative vibes." I responded to her criticism of the coffee by requesting that she be "positive" and begin by saying something good about the coffee. Thinking for a moment Mother retorted: "This coffee would make good creosote for fence posts." It was a start, and she began to grow a positive attitude.

It was good to see her grow and develop in her later years. The last decade of life was lived in a lovely apartment, surrounded by friends. They walked together daily in the mall, rode the same bus to church, and often traveled places together. One of her friends accompanied her twice to Oxford, England. By the time she passed at age 91, she had a bright and positive outlook about both the present and the future. Her last words were: "I am not afraid; I am ready to go."

77   MY PARENTS MET AT SCHOOL

Recently I drove by to show my wife the old schoolhouse where my parents met. I was disappointed: the school house was gone and in its place was a home. I thought how appropriate for a home to replace the school.

In 1926, Mother was teaching in the Carpe Grammar School when a young man in a green coat visited her class to see his cousin. Mother introduced the stranger as "Mr. Green" because of his coat not knowing that her description was in fact his real surname. That chance meeting was the beginning of a relationship which produced a home and three children: Betty, Hollis, and Wilma Sue "Susanne." As I think back, it is good that a home stands on the spot as a silent witness to other chance meetings that produced all the good virtues of home and family. Maybe there is a message for all of us.

The school can never replace the home. In these days of "home schooling," the home has literally replaced the school house. I am not convinced that home schooling should replace the public school, but I am sure that the school would be better if more attention were given to the needs of the children by the parents in the home. In fact, government studies since the 1960's demonstrated that parental involvement in the school work of children was the most significant factor in predicting academic achievement.

78   A ONE ROOM SCHOOL

Early in her career, my mother was a teacher in a one room school. She had grades one - eight. It was a challenge, but probably the best education that America has provided for the elementary and secondary levels. In fact, the entrance exam given to eighth graders for access to high school was one that many college graduates could not pass today.

I asked Mother to explain the dynamics of the one room school. It was simple: the fast learners were able to be challenged by listening to the upper class lessons, and the slow learners were able to review difficult lessons by hearing them taught to lower grades. Also the older and smarter students became teachers for the younger. Everyone benefited from the process. Individuals were prepared for life and higher education in the one room school.

Mother shared that one particular boy in her class seemed to read diligently when the group read their lessons aloud, but he never knew the material. As a teacher, Mother was concerned. She arranged with the rest of the class to stop reading at a given signal so she could hear the one student read aloud. She learned why he didn't know the lesson; He was reading aloud, "Here, Tag, here, Tag, here, Tag, . . . " He was simply calling his dog.

The one room school worked for most students, except those who spent time calling their dog or for some students who "do not pay attention." In fact, I remember an excuse given to me for a person's poor academic performance; he said, "I was so poor; I couldn't pay attention."

On another occasion three brothers were late for school on a snowy day and from their clothing they had obviously been playing around in the snow. When they finally arrived the oldest boy explained, "Miss Curton, sorry we are late, it was so slick out there...every time we took a step toward school we slid back two toward home."

Mother asked the logical question, "Well, tell us how you finally got to school." Without hesitation the answer was, "We got mad and started home." Mother said she could not bear to punish such a bright young lad. Oh, for the good old days when the teachers understood the students and the students were mostly honest and without excuses. In fact, Mother taught me the meaning of an "excuse." Her definition was "An excuse is the skin off a reason stuffed with a lie."

79   BOSS THE SECOND 50 YEARS

It was a cold and rainy day (December 29, 1901), when my paternal grandparents were married. Across from the church, the creek was up. I remember hearing the story of how the modest maiden let her wedding dress get wet going across the creek rather than let her husband-to-be see her ankle.

During the buggy ride to church, my paternal Grandfather, Alexander Little Page Green, (1874-1963), made a bargain. It was a good, fair, and equitable arrangement; Grandfather told his bride-to-be, "If you let me be the boss the first 50 years, you can be the boss the next 50 years." With humility the young bride agreed. What else could she do?

Surely Grandfather had not expected to reach the 50-year mark. After the whole family celebrated their 50th Wedding Anniversary, my Grandmother, Mattie Barton Green, (1883-1966), remembered her promise and Grandfather's bargain. She became the boss, at least, in name and spirit.

One Sunday I remember in particular because it was raining, and Grandfather didn't want to go to church. She ordered him out of bed, saying, "Doc Green, it was raining the day we got married and that didn't slow you down. I'm the boss now, and you and I are going to church."

I will always remember Grandfather's response, "A bargain is a bargain." After that, Grandmother even made him go fishing from time to time just to prove she was the boss. She would say, "You work too hard. A man of your age should relax more; I am the boss, and I say you must go fishing. We haven't had a good mess of fish in weeks." Grandfather willingly obeyed...she was the boss! I guess it is nice to have a good boss.

80 DIFFERENT KINDS OF BISCUIT EATERS

Grandfather Green would not eat regular biscuits. Grandmother had to fry a hoe-cake in a skillet on top of the stove especially for him three times a day. He claimed that baking powder made him sick. So Grandmother had to buy plain flour, and this complicated her cooking. Sometimes she would buy self-rising flour and put in a plain flour sack to placate Grandfather's peculiar attitude about biscuits.

On one occasion Grandfather found out her secret and got sick. Grandmother said, "Doc Green, you've been eating self-rising flour for three months, and you didn't get sick until you found this sack. It is in your mind. I am not playing this game anymore. You eat what I cook, or I will feed it to the dogs." She still made him a hoe-cake on top of the stove, but he didn't know if it was made with plain or self-rising flour. I guess if there are people who like different kinds of biscuits, there must be different kinds of biscuit makers. In fact, scripture declared, "8. When you are welcomed in any place, eat what is set before you," (Luke 10:8 DNT).

81   WEDDING RING IN THE GARDEN

My paternal Grandmother Green was a saint. She loved God, her husband, her children, her grandchildren, and practiced her faith on a daily basis. The loss of her wedding ring while gardening was a blow. There was no money to buy another ring; she wanted the one used in her wedding ceremony. Nothing else would satisfy her.

A year of praying and fretting about her wedding band passed until one day, William, her oldest son, was digging in the garden and found a little piece of gold. Rushing to his mother with his marvelous find, the clod of dirt was removed, and it was washed clean. It was gold...a gold ring. A "whoop and a holler" reverberated from the kitchen that could be heard on the next three farms. Grandmother had her wedding band. Her life was a little brighter after that day. William was excited too that his mother was so happy. He didn't understand all the ramifications of finding gold in the garden, but he was happy just the same.

Children do not always clearly understand all that goes on in the heart and soul of parents. However, during the many weddings I have conducted during my years in ministry, the act of consecrating the wedding ring for the bride always brought memories of Grandmother's precious wedding band. I also remember the joy of discovery enjoyed by William.

82   PROUD OF HIS CROP

My Grandfather Green was a faithful Methodist who believed and trusted in God. He was primarily a farmer and an amateur herbalist and horticulturist. One Sunday after church he showed his distinguished crop of corn to a visiting city slicker. The fellow thought Grandfather was too proud of his own labors and told him to be grateful to God for providing the soil, the sunshine, and the rain. He said that in reality it was God who made the corn grow. After listening to the exhortation, my grandfather retaliated, "I know God is working, but you should have seen that field when God had it by Himself! He sure left a lot of work for me."

83   PAPA IS GOING TO KILL US

The men in the Green family enjoyed hunting, especially in the winter. One day a group of my uncles and cousins went rabbit hunting near Pikeville, Tennessee. Together they killed 128 rabbits. As the cars were returning from the hunt loaded with tired hunters and trunks full of rabbits, one uncle remembered his father's rule concerning the killing of wildlife. "What you kill you must eat. Only kill what you need to eat." The uncle exclaimed, "Papa is going to kill us!" Another uncle continued, "How are we going to eat 128 rabbits? Papa is going to kill us!"

The group decided to drive through the little town and give away all the rabbits they could. There were 76 left. They stopped by a few friends' houses and eliminated 10 or 12 more. "What are we going to do?" One of the men suggested, "Our wives will just have to can them." And this they did. All night they skinned, steamed, boiled, and fried rabbits. Finally they were down to just a few. Someone said, "Let's give them to Papa!" Good idea.

By now it was early morning, almost breakfast time. When they arrived at the house, Grandmother was cooking rabbit for breakfast. I honestly don't know whatever happened to the rest of the rabbits. Probably the dogs had a feast. It was a lesson learned.

This lesson was so engrained in my subconscious that I was always afraid to mess with guns: I guess that's why I never wanted to be a Policeman or go to war. I live on top of a mountain where there are lots of animals, but since I don't eat wild meat, the animals are safe, at least from me.

84   HONEY, HAVE SOME

There was always honey on Grandmother Green's table. When a guest was present, especially a lady, Grandfather always pulled this one. He would pass the honey jar and say to the lady, "Honey? Have some." If the lady got the message and smiled, Grandfather would pick up the sugar bowl and ask, "Sugar? For your coffee?" There are several other such sayings, but they don't come to mind just now. I'll think of them in the shower next week.

85   IT SURE IS WORTH IT

Some distant relative of my Grandmother Green was free-loading. He stayed for long periods and would nearly eat them out of house and home. Grandmother would trade extra eggs and butter in town for other things she needed. There wasn't much cash in those days. The free-loader would eat globs of butter on his biscuit.

One morning Grandmother took all she could and said, "Butter is sure expensive," and she mentioned the price per pound. The free-loader took notice of her concern, but reached for another helping of freshly churned country butter and said, "Butter is expensive, but it sure is worth every penny." Grandfather would usually have to step in and explain to the free-loading kin that they had over stayed their welcome. It was hard to do, but necessary if Grandmother would have any butter and eggs left for trading in town.

86 A VISIT TO THE SMOKEHOUSE

As a grown man, I returned to the house where my Grandfather Green had lived. I visited the old smoke house. Someone had gathered up all the old tools and tack from the barn and placed it there for safe keeping. Observing the old smokehouse, I thought 'if this place burns much of this would be lost.' I backed my car up to the smokehouse and loaded my trunk with Grandfather's stuff.

The next week the home place and the old smokehouse burned to the ground. It was a great joy to distribute the stuff I had saved to my cousins. I still have some of the things: a carpenter's level, the saddle bags used by grandfather's brother who was a Medical Doctor, the heavy iron weight that kept the gate open, some tools from the farm's blacksmith shop, a bee smoker, and a few carpenter's tools. These items are not worth much on the market, but no one in the world has enough money to buy them. I wonder if anyone will want my stuff the way I enjoy my grandfather's things.

87   DADDY WAS GOOD WITH CARS

When my grandfather bought his first automobile, a
T-Model Ford, his oldest son, William, logically had the
seniority to be Grandfather's driver. My father was
the second son and was both excited about the auto and
somewhat knowledgeable of how it worked. My father would
slip out and take a wire off some part of the engine so it
would not start. The next morning, Grandfather would be
ready to go so William would crank the car, and crank, and
crank, but it would not start.

Grandfather would say, "Somebody get Barton!" Daddy
would crank a time or two, then go to the engine and fiddle
around a little putting the wire back in place. The engine
would crank, and Grandfather would say, "Barton, you'd
better drive today and keep this thing running." I don't
know if William ever figured out Daddy's strategy or not. It
amazes me that little things such as that are remembered
after all these years.

I remember two additional stories about Daddy and cars.
One relates to a long hill near Soddy Lake. If a car could
pull that long hill in high gear, Daddy thought it was a good
car. When I bought my first car, a 1939 Plymouth, I tested
it on that hill. It pulled the hill in high gear, so I bought it.
Even today when I drive up that hill I consciously listen to
the engine and wonder if this car had a stick shift would it
pull this hill in high gear.

The other is about finding a parking place. As Chattanooga
grew with more cars, it became difficult to find a parking
place. My father would become disturbed and say, "It
takes 14 gallons of gas to find a parking place." If he were
alive, I can't imagine what he would say about the price of
gasoline?

88 THEY BUILT MOTHER A HOUSE

When my father died in 1937, Mother was left with three small children: ages nine, four, and six months. We lived in Chattanooga, but Mother could not work and care for the baby so she decided to move to Rhea County to be close to family. My Grandfather Green and Grandfather Curton worked together; one provided the lumber, and the other, with the help of Daddy's brothers, built Mother and the children a house.

The house still stands as a memorial to family concern and care. When the family moved back to Chattanooga, Aunt Bettie, who cared for Mother during pregnancy, moved into the house. It was a natural process for the house to become the home for Bettie when she married Buster Jones. They lived there until their deaths.

Each time I pass this house, I remember the support the family gave my mother at the untimely death of Daddy at age 30. All of those who built that house have joined Daddy in death, but the house still stands as a testimony that family is important and that members of families must stand together during the best of times and the worst of times.

89 LET ME TELL YOU ABOUT YOUR FATHER

In 1982 I received a letter from Robert Adams. He saw my name in Who's Who and noted that I was born in Rhea County to Barton and Grace Green. He shared that in 1937 he was being mentored by a man from Mountain Creek Baptist Church named Barton who died suddenly. "He had a young son with an odd name, could that be you? If you are the son of Barton Green, let me tell you about your father."

Bob Adams had been on General MacArthur's staff, worked in a number of colleges, and was approaching retirement. He described my father as a genuine Christian and told of his efforts to disciple young men in the Chattanooga area. Daddy had encouraged him to go to college and do something good with his life. Finally, I was able to meet with Bob, and he shared many things about Daddy that I didn't know. It was good that Daddy was remembered for his service.

90   YOUR DADDY WOULD BE PROUD

Fifty years after my father's death, I was in a barbershop waiting to get a haircut. I was being observed by an older gentleman. When I walked to the barber's chair, the man came to the chair and spoke to me. "I'm sure of it now. When you walked to the chair, you looked just like Barton Green." When I told him that Barton was my father, he responded, "Barton was a Christian gentleman! What kind of work do you do?" Sharing that I was a preacher and a professor, the man responded, "Your daddy would be proud."

91   DUCKS IN A ROW

When I gave up my academic position at another institution and started a graduate school, Mother was upset. She said, "You will spend your fortune, and nobody will appreciate what you have done." Explaining that it was not a one man project and that others were assisting with the development of the new school, Mother was not convinced.

She saw building plans, books, and people everywhere doing she didn't know what. She exclaimed, "I hope I live to see you get all your ducks in a row!" At the first Graduation Exercises (July, 1984) as I marched in with faculty, staff, graduating class, and student body, we were all dressed in robes and marching in file. Mother turned to my sister and said, "Well, I guess he got his ducks in a row after all!"

Sometime later individuals from 38 countries and 72 denominations have graduated with either a Master's Degree or a Doctor of Philosophy. These good men and women are making a difference around the world in various positions. Although I am retired having served as President, Chancellor, and Distinguished Professor of Education and Social Change, I am pleased with the process and the product. Others now must carry the torch. I wish them all God's Speed!

Yes, I said "retired," but in the truest sense that word is not in my vocabulary. My Grandfather Green told me, "Never retire. When old folk get tired of doing nothing they can't stop and rest. And that's why old folk die!" I still enjoy traveling, speaking, writing books, teaching at OASIS UNIVERSITY, and serving as Chair of Global Educational Advance, Inc. [www.globaledadvance.org], and Publisher of GlobalEdAdvancePress. Check it out. [www.gea-books.com] Buy some books!

92   GLASSES, WHETSTONE, AND CANE

My father, Herbert Barton Green, (1907-1937), died when I was four. Sometimes I remember him, but it is probably things that others told me about him. As a child, my family constantly told me about my father. How brave he was in going to get the cow up a dark hallow and whistling all the way. He was good with a rifle. He enjoyed cars. He always wanted to be dressed up, neat, and clean. He was very religious.

Daddy had rheumatic fever as a child and was told that he would not live to see manhood. He married Grace Irene Curton (1905-1996) and fathered three children: Betty Jo (Stout), Hollis Lynn, and Wilma Sue (Susanne Faust). His widow survived him by 59 years. Betty also passed, but the other two are still kicking; Hollis at 79 and Susanne at 75.

The fever affected his heart; he was only 30 when he died, October 8, 1937. I have only three things that were his: a pair of gold rimmed glasses, a whet stone for which he carved a wooden box with his name on it, and a walking stick with his initials carved for all to see. Each item is precious to me and conjures up various images and ideas about my father. Most of all I think they speak to me of things he would want me to know.

The glasses he wore everyday say, "Look daily at life; it is precious." Daddy had a philosophy which he called G.O.A.L., "Get Out And Live." See the roses and the beauty around you. See the world and don't let physical limitations stop you. He knew his life would be short, but it was filled with work, church, play, fishing, hunting, his wife, his children, his brothers, his sisters, and his friends. Although, Daddy passed 75 years ago, he is still remembered fondly by all who knew him.

The wooden box and whet stone were made during a 1924 trip to Hot Springs, Arkansas, to take hot baths and recover his strength. He used it regularly to keep his pocket knife sharp (I lost the knife when I was a child). What does the box and the whet stone say? Clearly, it points out that one's tools must be ready. It declares that honest work is good for the soul, and the box with the date and his name carved on it speaks to anyone and says, "I was here. What I did was important! Don't forget me."

In fact, his brothers have taken me to rocks and trees on which he carved his initials. He had a special way of carving on a tree. He made just one deep stroke into the bark of a tree with his knife and let the growth of the tree over time reveal his initials. On the rocks, he always went to the underneath side or the overhang protected from the weather. He wanted to be remembered. Those who carved out the letters so one could see them immediately had their initials soon disfigured by tree growth, but the growth over time just make Daddy's initials more prominent. "HBG was here; don't forget me!"

The walking stick was used in a forced effort to remain active and live up to his G.O.A.L. motto, "Get Out And Live." He was active. He worked the last day of his life, and took a car load of young men to a church service. Daddy came in after the family was asleep. With the baby in bed with Mother, Daddy hung his clothes on a chair, slipped into the foot of the bed in an effort not to disturb them, and died in his sleep.

The walking stick is useful. It assists and comforts me in times of need. After an operation and prior to and following knee surgery, Daddy's walking stick was used. With each step I could feel his hand escorting me forward. I could almost hear a soft voice saying, "Keep pushing, Son, and don't let it get you down."

I had two other personal mementos from my father: his pocket knife and his favorite 12 gage shot gun. The knife was lost when I was a child, and the gun was stolen some years ago on Christmas Eve. The loss was most painful. The gun had a mighty kick. I have a picture of the last turkey Daddy shot with that gun. Somewhere Daddy's bird gun is hanging over a mantle, but they don't know the stories that go with the gun nor do they know the man who owned and used the gun. (Down inside are the initials HBG, someday I may find it). The knife and the gun are gone, one through my childish carelessness, the other because of a thief. Even these lost items speak to me.

The knife reminds me to be careful with things that are dear and valuable. Thoughts of Daddy's gun remind me that there are still people in the world who are "takers" and that everyone must be watchful and protective of both property and heritage. The memories and the life Daddy lived are real.

93   A SAWMILL LUNCH

My maternal Grandfather, Robert Tate Curton, (1877-1955), was a timber man. He owned a sawmill and cut lumber. I didn't spend much time with my mother's side of the family. My father's family seemed to claim me as their very own and left little room for anyone else. That is not to be taken as a negative statement; it is just the facts related to the English history of the Greens. Consequently, effort had to be made to spend time with my Grandfather Curton.

On this occasion it was to travel to the back woods to a mountain sawmill. I could watch them cut trees; drag the logs with mules, horses, and tractors; and then at the sawmill watch them cut the logs into lumber.

My Grandmother, Ida Dobbs Curton, (1881-1962), made me a sack lunch. I placed it on a big rock. When dinner time came, the ants had already found the jelly and biscuits and had taken over the whole sack lunch. What was I to do? In the middle of nowhere, the closest Krystal hamburger was 60 miles away. I observed the others. They had taken string and tied their lunch bucket in a tree. It was in a bucket with a sealed lid. No ants could get their lunch.

Some shared with me, but most of them laughed at me for being so ignorant. Almost every time I go to the woods, I think of the sawmill lunch and how hungry I got that day in the middle of nowhere. I wasn't anxious to again visit the sawmill. That's too bad, too, because Mr. Curton, as his hands called him, was a warm and generous man - most of

the time. Somehow, sorry to say, there was hardly room in
my heart for two grandfathers.

94   CORNBREAD WAS ALL CORNERS

Mother often fixed brown cornbread for supper. We ate
it with milk, but my sister, Betty Jo, and I often fussed
over who would get the corners to crumble in our milk. When
Mother got tired of the hassle, she started using a round pan
to bake the cornbread. She put the bread on the table and
said, "Now, it's all corners!" I still enjoy brown cornbread,
the corners, the edges, and milk. I wish it were all corners.

95   PLANTING A LIVE CHRISTMAS TREE

My sons are grown and have a life of their own. Some
years ago when both were home for Christmas, we bought a
live tree to replant after the holidays. Before the boys left,
we dug a hole and planted the tree. It grows today in Green
Oaks Park on the campus of Oxford Graduate School. Each
Christmas we decorate it with lights and let them burn for
the pleasure of the faculty, staff, students, and the lonely
passerby.

As I watch the tree grow and as I decorate it each year,
I am reminded of the good times when the boys were small
and could appreciate Christmas and all that it means for
family and faith. Both boys are busy now: one is a big time
author and the other is an actor on Broadway. I am proud
of them both, but I will always remember that Christmas we
planted the tree together. I will also endeavor to keep it
alive by decorating the living tree each year. Life is short.
One must make the most of each pleasure and hold on to the
meaningful memories in a life much too short.

96   THE PROBLEM OF BISCUIT MAKERS

There are two kinds of biscuit makers in the world: those who cook fat white biscuits [my mother-in-law, Lucille Parks] and the thin brown biscuit makers [my mother, Grace Green]. Let me share the story about a marriage conflict over biscuits. It seems this couple had been recently married and was sitting at the breakfast table. The wife normally cooks biscuits the way her mother did. The husband looked at the wife and asked, "Why did you burn the biscuits?" She answered, "I didn't burn the biscuits." Naturally the discussion continued with the repeating of the question and the repeating of the answer until the bitter argument brought about separation and finally divorce. One day the couple got back together, remarried, and sat down at the table and began to discuss the foolishness of their separation. The husband said, "Wasn't it foolish for us to get divorced just because you burned the biscuits?" She said, "I didn't burn the biscuits." You can guess the rest of the story.

97   AM I REALLY MARRIED?

My sister Betty Jo married a sailor just home from the war. George Stout had been out of the Navy just a few weeks when they married. The church where the family attended was building a new building, but it wasn't completed. Services were held in a Gospel Tent next to the new construction. There was a saw dust floor and home-made, very uncomfortable benches.

With no money for flowers and big wedding stuff, George and Betty were married at the close of the Sunday morning worship service. The Pastor had the congregation sing "Where He Leads Me I will Follow." George and Betty stood in the saw dust at the altar. The minister's wedding service was extremely short, and the couple was off to Gatlinburg for their honeymoon. George, just home from the War, had not purchased a car, so they were to travel by Greyhound.

I will always remember accompanying them to the Bus Station and Betty leaning out the window to ask Mother a question. Being brought up by a strict mother, Betty was concerned about going off with a Sailor, after such an informal and short service. She actually wondered about the validity of the ceremony. Betty was having real doubts that everything that had been so wrong before was somehow made right by this brief ceremony. Her question, "Mother, are we really married?" Mother assured her that they were legally married and that "everything" was legal and proper.

George and Betty had a good marriage that produced four well educated and talented children: two boys and two girls. I am still amazed how strangers can meet, fall in love, marry, have children, and generally have a wonderful life. Marriage seems such a risky venture, but somehow it works to the benefit of society. Isn't it wonderful how God's blessings and the sanction of the Christian community brings correctness to a relationship and opens the door to such fruitful lives?

98   THE PARKING LOT HUG

My wife and I came upon a middle age couple embracing fervently in a restaurant parking lot. You could not tell if it was a "hello" or "a good bye" event. As we approached, the hugging stopped. Passing them, I said, "Every time I get in a hugging line it stops." Hearing my comment the woman ran, grabbed me, and nearly squeezed the life out of me. My wife stood amazed, and I felt a little flushed.

The couple was not married. She was returning to her hometown to get a parrot she had left with friends.

She planned to return for the wedding. Learning this, I
commented that he had lost his chick to a bird. A few weeks
later I saw the gentlemen and asked about the bride-to-be.
He said, "The bird won!" I guess it was a "good bye hug!"

99   CHANGE OF PACE NEEDED

My Uncle John Edward Green told me of two friends who
worked in a stressful job in a busy city. They decided to
take early retirement and buy a place in the country and do
some less stressful task. They bought a farm and began a
process of elimination to determine what kind of "farmers"
they would be. They decided on a chicken farm. The County
Agent surveyed the buildings and land and told them they
could accommodate 300 chickens. They ordered the baby
chicks.

Three weeks later they returned to the County Agent and
wanted more baby chicks. "Your place is not big enough for
more than 300 chickens," said the agent. "Well we need
to re-order. We must have planted them too deep because
they didn't come up."

The County Agent suggested that they search for another
kind of farming. In doing so they noticed a man plowing a
garden with his mule. They stopped and discussed farming
with the man and asked them where they could buy a mule.
The farmer said it was best to hatch their own so it would
become adjusted to their lifestyle and told them they could
get a "mule egg" from a farmer down the road who would also
tell them how to hatch it.

They found the farmer and asked for a mule egg. The
farmer gave them a large stripped watermelon and told them
they would have to sit on it for six weeks, 24 hours a day
to hatch it. On the way home, carrying the watermelon and
discussing a schedule for taking turns sitting on the egg,

one stumbled. They dropped the watermelon, and it burst
into some bushes and up jumped a rabbit. As the rabbit
scampered up the path, one said to the other, "Look there
you have lost our mule!" The other said, "Seeing how fast a
baby mule can run, I don't think we would want to work that
fast anyway. We better find some other kind of farming."

100   WASH MY CAR

One of my father's brothers, John Edward Green, (1915-
1989), had a 1941 Ford Convertible. It was tan and hardly
showed dust, but my uncle would say to me, "My car really
needs washing. Why don't you drive it to the branch and
wash it for me?" He knew how I loved cars.

My mother didn't have a car and this gesture of concern
for me, that produced my joy of driving and washing the car,
sometime twice a day in the summer, was something special.
In hindsight it was such a nice thing to do for a 12 year old
without a father or a car. I had learned to shift gears on
a farm tractor, but driving a Ford convertible was a blast.
Most of my memories of Uncle Edward related to his love for
cars, trucks, and me. It was a joy to remember such events
at his funeral service. He was my kind of man!

If I happen to see an old Ford convertible on the road,
a feeling of great joy comes over me. A few weeks ago
driving near Gatlinburg, several old Fords passed by going to
an antique car show. It brought back such good memories of
Uncle Edward and his tan convertible and the easy job I had
washing it on a dusty day.

101   I HAD TO GROW A BEARD

When my oldest son, Barton, was a teenager, he wanted
to grow a beard. I asked him not to because of the hippie

issue at the time. I wanted to avoid criticism of the family from members of the church. Bart said, "What's wrong with growing a beard? Jesus wore a beard." Of course, Jesus wore a beard; he also wore sandals and walked everywhere he went, too. "If having a beard is not wrong, why don't you grow one, dad?"

My response included a promise that I would grow a beard when I was older. The question was at what age. We agreed on age 50. Years passed, and a few weeks before my 50th birthday, Bart began calling my wife. Has dad started his beard yet? A negative answer would elicit a response, such as, "Well, I know he will, because dad has always kept his word to me." I had no choice but to grow a beard.

I did grow a beard for my 50th birthday to keep my word. I went to the studio and had pictures taken of the full beard and promptly shaved it. Sending a photo to my son to prove I had kept my word seemed to settle the issue, but it didn't. My wife liked the beard. My mother didn't. Some thought I looked older, others younger. It was mostly grey.

Every year or so I would grow a beard over the Thanksgiving/Christmas holiday and wear it to my annual seminars in Oxford, England, each January. My English friends thought the beard made me look more professorial. Since that was my job, the beard finally stuck. My official photograph as Chancellor of Oxford Graduate School, American Centre for Religion/Society Studies, was with full beard. By age 60 the beard was permanent.

102   MOTHER DIDN'T LIKE WHISKERS

My mother knew a beard only as whiskers. She remembered the old men who didn't shave and looked rather woolly. She expressed a definite dislike for my beard. I explained that a beard was different than whiskers. A beard normally requires shaving each day and regular trimming.

Nothing seemed to help Mother accept her son in a beard. "You just don't look like yourself," she would comment. Finally, I said, "I am no longer a pastor or Military Chaplain, where beards were unacceptable. I am now a professor, and people expect a professor to look weird and crazy. Most people think it makes me look more professorial." After some time, Mother, attempting to make a concession in her feelings, one day said, "Well, I guess you look better in a beard that anybody I have seen before." At last, I had Mother's approval.

103 YOU SPOKE AT MY GRADUATION

A few years ago I was scheduled to speak at a college commencement in Florida. A local resident saw my photo in the paper and located me at the Holiday Inn. In an English accent, he asked to have breakfast the next morning. When he arrived, I was surprised to see he was black. He said, "Dr. Green, you may not remember me, but you spoke at my college commencement thirty-four years ago." I remembered the occasion in Jamaica, but not the individual. He continued, "I even remember your address." I was flattered that he remembered both me and the address. He said, "You spoke three times in St. Mary's Parish, and I remember those sermons, too. Do you remember that I barrowed and read your books?"

The young men of the college in Jamaica were so eager to learn that they remembered almost everything anyone said to them in the context of the school. Thinking back, I remembered one of the students who asked if I had any books with me. I did have three or four in my briefcase.

He asked to read them. When I asked which one, he said all
of them.

The next morning at breakfast, the student said, "I have
finished all the books, but my roommate still needs time to
finish the last one. Would it be O.K. if he kept them until
lunch?" At lunch the student asked if others in the dorm
could read the books. Before I left that campus many
of the ministerial students had read the books from my
briefcase. I had never witnessed such hunger for knowledge.

Returning to the states, I shipped 500 volumes from
my personal library to the school library. It was a good
investment. Also, the next pastor's conference I attended,
the participants were asked to bring two books from their
personal library appropriate for ministerial students. We
shipped another 1,200 books.

One of those students was Frank O. duCille, who became a
specialist in small Church development, maintained an interest
in missionary work in Jamaica, and continued in a pastorate
even after his retirement. He died May 6, 1998, while
attending a conference on small Church development.

Frank lived to be seventy-three (73) and died with his
boots on. To remember Frank and the others who have
given so much, we built an extension to the Campus Chapel
at Oxford Graduate School. It is called "The duCille Alcove
on the Chapel Court" and is a constant reminder to faculty,
staff, and students of the unfinished work of the Great
Commission.

104   THE TRUCK LOAD OF WATERMELONS

I just returned from my annual Green Reunion. Usually
there is a truck load of free watermelons by Uncle Henegar's
place. The absence of the free watermelons spoke volumes

to me about deteriorating health and the aging process. I
often saw Uncle Henegar working in his garden. He was
nearly 90 years old, but still working at growing things.
Maybe there was a problem with the crop this year. I will
look for his watermelons next year and every year in the
future. He seemed to get such joy in giving away his juicy
watermelons. They were a generous statement about hard
work and sharing the bounty with others. There are always
lessons to be learned from the small deeds done by others.
If watermelons could talk, we would hear some juicy stories.

The last year Uncle Henegar brought watermelons to
the family reunion, I saved seeds and passed them out the
next year. Those present were asked to plant, cultivate,
and bring melons to the next reunion. It is good to keep a
tradition alive, especially if it means good watermelon on a
hot day.

105 BULOVA AND CARPENTER DOGS

I went with my Uncle William to visit a man who had
lots of dogs running loose in the yard. They seemed to
be all different breeds and sizes. When asked what kind
of dogs he had, he replied, "I have two kinds: Bulova and
Carpenter dogs." We had never heard of such breeds. The
fellow explained, "The Bulova dogs are watch dogs, and the
Carpenter dogs do little odd jobs around the place."

106 WHEN YOUR LAST PARENT DIES

I was scheduled to speak in a Community Church in
Maryland and was staying with some new friends. He was
a graduate dean and a statistics professor, and she was
a Medical Doctor. We had some long conversations about
various subjects. Mostly we talked about two of my books,

Why Churches Die and Why Christianity Fails in America. One asked why the negative approach to the subject? I explained that it was diagnostic and that I had lived long enough and learned enough to speak plainly about observed problems with the church. The Professor said, "My wife has that same attitude. At what age does one abandon caution, develop a damn the torpedoes mindset, and go full speed ahead?"

Without thinking my answer was, "When your last parent dies. As long as one parent lives, you are a child, but when the last one passes things change. You are no longer a child. You have to face your own mortality and step up to the plate, take responsibility, and tell it like it is. You now must speak to the next generation and share what you have learned. What you do you must do quickly and with conviction." His response was encouraging, "I believe you are right. My wife did change when her father died."

My mother passed in 1996; she was almost 92, and her passing changed my perspective. After her death, I was compelled to restart my writing career that had been placed on hold to establish a graduate school. I am now working on book number 48. My goal is to write 50 books before I pass on. I believe each individual has a responsibility to pass on to the next generation lessons learned and problems identified. When a person dies, it's like a library has burned to the ground - all that information lost unless it is written down and published.

107　TRAVIS, WHAT ARE YOU DOING?

A young man was working in the Chapel garden at Oxford Graduate School. He was told to work quietly because it was a sacred place and that God might speak to him while he was near the chapel. The garden is below the high wall of the chapel court. I was standing above the garden at the high wall, and Travis was slowly working below. I was surprised that my question, "Travis, what are you doing?" startled him so. Later, he explained that he was thinking, "What if God speaks to me? What will I say? Then I heard my name... 'TRAVIS,' from above...I thought God was calling my name."

108   THE WORST COFFEE

My mother, Grace Curton Green, (1905-1996), was born to hard times and experienced World War I, the Great Depression, the death of a young husband at age 31, experienced World War II, and raised and educated three children as a single parent. When my father died in 1937, he was not yet invested in Social Security. It was natural that she would develop a harsh and negative view of life. One day Mother and I were drinking coffee in a small shop, and she commented, "This is the worst coffee I have ever had!" The comment was made loud enough for most in the small shop to hear.

I was struggling to begin a new graduate school and trying to remain positive in my general attitude. It was difficult, during those days, to be around Mother without some "negative vibes." I responded to her criticism of the coffee by requesting that she be "positive" and begin by saying something good about the coffee. Thinking for a moment Mother retorted: "This coffee would make good creosote for fence posts." It was a start, and she began to grow a positive attitude.

It was good to see her grow and develop in her later years. The last decade of life was lived in a lovely apartment, surrounded by friends. They walked together daily in the mall, rode the same bus to church, and often traveled places together. One of her friends accompanied her twice to Oxford, England. By the time she passed at age 92, she had a bright and positive outlook about both the present and the future. Her last words were: "I am not afraid; I am ready to go." This is a "so tale" which I shared at her funeral.

SECTION THREE

Domestic and Foreign Travel

109   TRAVELING I LOOK FOR ART BARGAINS

I have always been interested in art. My early drawings won me a scholarship as a commercial cartoonist, but I never took advantage of the opportunity to study formally. However, as a self-taught artist I work with acrylics to produce some acceptable work and give them as gifts, but sell a few. Mostly, I paint landscape scenes and rare or near extinct animals. Usually there are no people in my paintings because I suffer from "people fatigue" as both a minister and a professor. My oldest son recently visited one of the colleges in Oxford, UK. While waiting in the outer office to see my friend, Geoffrey Thomas, the secretary pointed to a painting and said, "Your father painted that picture." Surprised, Bart looked closely, and there was the tell-tale signature, "Hollis." All my paintings are signed simply "HOLLIS" with a date. If you run across paintings that one of my friends sold, buy it even in a flea market. It will probably be worth lots of money after I'm dead.

Back in the 1960's I went with a friend, David Bishop, to an Art Exhibit in Los Angeles. He was a painter, so I asked that he select something for me to purchase. He located a beautiful work titled, Study Number 2. It was colorful, had good design, and was in an extraordinarily nice frame. The price was also within my budget. I told the monitor at the exhibit that I wanted to purchase the painting and was told it was "Not for sale!" I protested that it had a price on it and was told that was for the frame only. Since some of the paintings designated such limitations and this one did not, I insisted on purchasing the painting. The monitor said he would call the artist.

I waited over an hour for the artist to travel across Los Angeles. When she arrived, I was questioned. "Are you a dealer? Do you plan to keep the painting for yourself?

Where will you hang it? What is your occupation?" followed
by many more questions. Finally, the artist said, "This
painting is of my husband. It has won design awards in three
showings. I have Study No. 1 hanging over my bed at home.
The painting is not for sale. The price is for the frame;
however, if you will agree to my terms I will let you have it
for that price."

The terms were simply: not to sell it during the artist's
lifetime, to hang it in a place of honor, and never show it
without a direct light attached to the frame or a spot from
the ceiling. I agreed. She sold me the painting. It hung
for years in my home library/study. Today it hangs in my
retirement home on Lone Mountain together with paintings
collected from around the world.

Each time I see Study No. 2, I am reminded of both the
terms of the negotiations that secured the painting and the
enjoyment it has brought to me over these many years. My
gratitude also goes to David for his expertise. Someday
I may even add one of David's paintings to my collection.
Probably after my rich Uncle gets out of the poor house.

110   I INSULTED THE MAID

Early in my ministry I visited a missionary in Jamaica.
He showed me around the island and explained many of the
customs. We attended some religious services, visited some
local politicians, and went to the straw market. Jamaica is a
beautiful place full of history and tradition.

There was a young native lady working in the missionary's
home. She served meals, cleaned, and watched after the
children and the house and grounds. One morning she was
not present to serve us breakfast. The next morning she
returned, and I commented, "I missed you yesterday." This
was obviously not a proper comment from an American to

make to a native girl. She awkwardly explained that she had gone to the country to visit her mother. I retorted that my guess was that she had gone to visit a boyfriend. She was shocked and hurt by this assumption and made an effort to explain.

"I am a Christian," she said with emphasis. "I do not have a boyfriend!" After she left the room, my missionary friend explained to me that I had just insulted her. Christian young people in Jamaica did not date or meet with the opposite sex without permission and supervision. I had just accused her by my assumption of being a loose woman and suggested she was sexually active. I was much more careful after that episode in my dealing with people in other cultures. It was a lesson I needed to learn. I never cease to be amazed at how words and actions mean different things in various cultures.

111   JUST MARRIED IN JAMAICA

In the 1960's some Jamaican churches still practiced the arranged marriage for parishioners. These churches did not permit social dating among marriage age young people. A man of age would select three (3) possible brides and give the list to the minister. The minister would speak with the young women in order of the list. If the first said "No" to the proposal, the minister would go to the next one and on down the list.

If all rejected the prospect of marriage to the young man, the minister would normally go to the parents of the first woman and attempt to persuade them to influence their daughter to marry this particular worthy young man. If unsuccessful, the minister would continue down the list. Should all refuse, the minister would ask for another list.

I spoke at a local college Sunday service and was invited home for Sunday dinner by a couple who had just married the evening before. They had never corresponded or spoken privately with one another until the wedding ceremony. The groom was a teacher in the college and owned a home. The bride had come from a church across the island. She prepared a fine Sunday meal for me. In addition to the surprise of being invited so early in their married life, I was amazed at the dining arrangements.

There was a long, narrow refectory table with benches on each side and a single chair at each end. The new bride seated me on one of the long benches, but moved both of the chairs and seated the couple on one of the narrow ends. Coming out of the American courtship approach to marriage, it was a real joy to see two people so much in love. Each movement, each bite of food, and each word was a joy to the other.

It made me wonder if the Western custom of emotionally selecting a mate without the advice of family and assistance of the church was the best approach. In the Western system of courtship, little was left for the honeymoon, but in this arranged marriage everything was new and exciting. It was a beautiful sight to see! I now understand that Jamaica has abandoned this practice and taken up more American ways. This has greatly altered their marriage and divorce statistics. Jamaicans now marry younger and divorce is more common as they take a more emotional approach to relationships. When something works, why do people want to change it? I clearly remember MGen. Jerry R. Curry telling me, "Don't fix what ain't broke!"

112   I SWAM IN DISCOVERY BAY

Traditionally Columbus discovered Jamaica by sailing into a particular bay, now called Discovery Bay. I had an opportunity to go swimming at this particular place and was excited to swim out into the bay to a large rock. Climbing out of the water onto the rock, I noticed a fine green moss above the water line. It so happened that I was allergic to this particular moss, and everywhere it touched me I broke out in itching whelps: between my toes, on my hands, legs, and even my stomach where I had climbed out of the water. In the heat, the itching was almost unbearable. There were no convenience stores or corner drug stores to buy medicine. I just had to endure the itching.

As I spoke in chapel at the college the next day, my toes began to itch. I had stuffed tissue paper between my toes in an attempt at relief. During my sermon my toes began to itch terribly, so I began stomping my feet . . . one and then the other. The young preachers in the Bible College thought I was getting happy so they joined in with shouts of "Glory," "Hallelujah," "Amen," etc. In all we had a good time. It sure beat some of the dry services I had been accustomed to in the good old USA.

113   THE MEXICAN CAR WASH

Traveling with some missionaries in Mexico, we stopped to eat. A boy of about 10 came up and asked permission to wash the windshield for a coin. When we agreed, he wanted to also wash the car. We agreed, but wondered where he would get the water. Mexico was especially dry that season.

We returned to a clean car with all the hubcaps shinning. When asked for an explanation about the water, we discovered the boy had washed the car with a Vienna sausage can of water and a handkerchief. He demonstrated putting the handkerchief in the small can of water, squeezing the water back into the can, spreading the cloth out, and pulling it across the car taking the dust away.

A wee bit of ingenuity, a little water, and a lot of brass will go a long way. I have often wondered what became of this miracle car wash boy. I trust his cleverness paid off. It certainly taught us a lesson about using what you have to get the job done. That boy, as a man, just might be the person who could save the world during the next worldwide drought. Since a large percentage of the world's population depends on rain water, we all could learn some conservation skills from this little boy's attitude and ingenuity. Water is precious and is necessary to operate almost everything; it actually costs more than gasoline when purchased by the gallon.

114 A PECKING ON THE WINDSHIELD

During my early travel I was driving my 1939 Plymouth coupe on old Route 11 in Virginia and fell asleep. In those days there was no money for hotels, so one normally kept on traveling or took a nap in the car. On this occasion, my mother was sick, and I was driving alone through the night. The monotonous road put me to sleep....on the windshield there was a pecking....peck, peck, peck. The noise awakened me. Two wheels were off the pavement and just ahead was a narrow bridge. I was saved by a peck on the windshield.

When this story was shared, some doubters said it was probably gravel thrown up from a passing car. I have always believed it was my Guardian Angel watching over me. Maybe it was Saint Somebody, or was it just Providence watching over a weary traveler on his way to visit a sick mother?

115 HOW DO YOU SPELL "WORLD RELIEF?"

Not long after Spiros Zodhiates moved his AMG, International from New Jersey to Chattanooga, Tennessee,

I attended a meeting where Dr. Zodhiates spoke. He was talking about his World Relief program and complaining that the people in Chattanooga couldn't spell. He turned to me, not realizing that I grew up in Chattanooga, and asked me, "Dr. Green, how do you spell relief?" My answer was simple and true,... "R-O-L-A-I-D-S."

After the meeting, I explained to Dr. Zodhiates why the people in the area were problem spellers. It seems that some years ago the University of Tennessee was experimenting with a new way to teach spelling. My fifth grade class at G. Russell Brown Elementary School was selected as subjects for the research. We were taught to spell by a new process called "sight memory" rather than sounding syllables. We could see a list of words and spell each one correctly by simply copying the word off our eye lids. The tragedy was that if we did not see a word for a while, we forget how to spell it. Later most of us had to teach ourselves to sound out the syllables, but at times we still don't trust ourselves and have to use a dictionary. Spell Check on computers has helped most of us. Well, anyway, my spelling of "relief" got a few laughs. And I got a dig at the fifth grade research project that "mesup my splin."

116   IS THAT MOTOR RUNNING?

Flying Delta into Cincinnati back in the prop days, the starboard engine caught fire. The pilot feathered the prop and applied the automatic fire extinguisher. During the process, the young stewardess hurried to the empty seat by me over the wing and asked, "Is that motor running?" Before I could answer, she continued, "Is the plane on fire?" Without taking a breath she asked, "Are you scared?" My answer was, "No, I'm ready to go!" She responded, "Go where?" "To Heaven," was my answer. With great frustration she said, "I wish I had time to talk to you."

The fire was out, and the plane landed safely. As I left the plane, she smiled and whispered, "Say a prayer for me." Hopefully, she prayed on her own. God does prompt by circumstance. Conscious of the possibility of disaster, when I fly, I wonder how many on the plane have made their peace with God.

This reminds me of a man who was afraid to fly. The story goes that his minister told him that no one would die until their time came. He asked, "What if the pilot's time comes, and it's not my time?" The obvious answer, "It pays to be ready."

117   WHY I LEARNED TO FLY

One summer I had a recurring dream. A number of times the dream included me being in a Spanish speaking country during a revolution or civil uprising, and there was no way to get out of the country. In my dream there was a small yellow airplane at a small air strip, and if I could fly that plane I could make it to the border. Then I would awake, to dream the same scenario again. The dream troubled me.

As a result of the dream I began to study Spanish and looked for someone to teach me to fly. After two years of Spanish, I could do OK conversationally, so I decided it was enough. Now, I must learn to fly. One day I asked a man at the Beckley Airport (WV) if he knew anyone who would teach me to fly. I was given a name and the location of a small sod air strip.

The instructor was an old pilot from World War II. After a few days of ground school, we began to fly. To make a long story much shorter, I did learn to fly, obtained my license, and began to rent, borrow, and "tag along" on every flight I could afford. The dreams stopped. I was now ready.

My travel has taken me into many Spanish speaking countries. On arrival I observe where the small planes are parked and ask how far and in what direction is the nearest border. In each case, I was ready in the event of a bloody revolution or civil war to go find a little yellow plane and fly to the border. Fortunately, it was never required, but I still have a few more trips to Spanish speaking counties left on the old ticker. You never know. If it happens, I will be ready, I think.

118   I SOLOED AFTER DARK

Learning to fly was fun, but the first time I flew by myself was an accident waiting to happen. It was late one day after a difficult flying lesson where the instructor had cut the engine at about 2,000 feet and said. "Find a place to land." When I located a possible site, he restarted the engine and said, "Let's practice landing on a cloud." He suggested that I pick out a cloud and bring the airplane to a landing stall on top of the cloud. I guess this was done, because the clouds were much softer than the ground, and gave some room for error. When this was attempted a few times, the instructor suggested that in an emergency one could land in the top of a large tree provided the pilot executed a landing stall just before settling into the tree top.

All of this talk had a purpose. After a couple of practice landings at the air strip, the instructor climbed out and said, "It's time for you to fly solo!" If this experienced pilot thought I was ready, there was no argument. Everything worked well until the landing pattern was almost completed, and I turned on the carburetor heat for the landing. A strong cross wind developed, and it became difficult to line up for the actual landing. I was too high and too fast, so I attempted a side slip maneuver, but because of the cross wind and my lack of experience, the plane simply picked up speed. I bounced hard two or three times and finally stopped.

The instructor rushed out to the plane and would not permit me to get out. If you don't go around again now, you will never fly again. Hurry, it's going to get dark. Turning the plane around and moving back to the starting place, I was so frightened I gave the throttle a pull and began my take off run without checking everything. In the excitement, I failed to turn off the carburetor heat. This caused the plane to be sluggish and take more time than normal to circle the pattern. By the time I was ready to make a final approach and reached for the carburetor heat, I realized what the problem had been. Because of the slow time around the pattern, it was now getting dark.

The field had no lights. I was in trouble. Continuing, I knew about where the field was from the sunlight on the mountain peaks; as I attempted to line up for a final, I saw lights. The instructor had arranged several vehicles on the field. I assumed the first two facing each other was the beginning of the runway and the next one was the touchdown stop. I was going to make it. It felt good to be on the ground.

119   I LOVED TO FLY SMALL PLANES, UNTIL...

It was always a joy to fly alone in a small plane with the radio off. It seemed so peaceful. It was great just to be away from the telephone. The fact that one must concentrate on the process of flying makes it difficult to worry or even think about other things. Flying always helped me recover from "people fatigue." It was my habit on a clear day to turn the radio off and just cruise around. This was a bad habit, because one day in South Florida three jets out of Homestead AFB overflew my small plane at lightning speed, passing me before I heard the sound.

The whole experience unnerved me. Flying was becoming a problem. A few days later I was about to enter the landing pattern in Moundsville, West Virginia, when a Piedmont Airline came in about 200 feet under a normal pattern and overflew my small plane. It was like the Queen Mary passing a row boat. I almost lost it! When I landed there were twigs and leaves stuck in the wheels.

The next morning, as I continued my flight toward Huntington the trim tab handle came off at the top of my climb. Holding the stick with my knees, I fished for my toolbox and some pliers to adjust the trim. As if that wasn't enough, the weather closed in on me. I was lost without instruments. I was in real trouble.

All I could do was put the plane in a 15 degree bank and circle downward hoping to locate a landmark before hitting some mountain. Finally, I saw a sign on a barn roof that oriented me, and I headed for the river and flew on to Huntington. The next day when I returned to the Beckley Airport, I told a friend, "I'm not going to fly anymore. I know just enough to get myself killed." My friend responded, "It really is hard to be a good pilot and be good at anything else." It was a lesson learned, but the time had come to go commercial. Although I lost the solitude of flying alone, actually going commercial provided many opportunities to share my faith. If my dream ever came true, and I was in a foreign country during a civil war, I would head for the airport and look for a little yellow plane. With confidence I would prop that sucker and head for the border.

120   THE SOLDIER CHOSE THE EMPTY SEAT

Traveling to Washington, D.C., during the Vietnam War to intercede for a young service man who had been mistreated because of his Christian faith, God opened a door for me to witness. Just before catching the plane, my schedule took me to a publisher to review the galley proof of a book. While there an old newspaper was noticed on the floor. Since neatness is a virtue, my decision was to pick up the paper. It had been used to cover an ink spill and was stuck to the floor. In the process, a small piece tore off in my hand. It was a picture of a skunk and a story about a farmer.

A Pennsylvania farmer had observed an old skunk for several days. One day the skunk abandoned his old home and dug a new nesting hole. The farmer was intrigued, so he watched. The skunk with great care gathered grass and leaves and lined the inside of the excavation. The skunk looked around for what was to be his last glance at the world, and then entered the hole. The behavior fascinated the farmer so he waited. When the skunk never came out of the hole, the farmer became curious.

Taking a stick, the farmer punched into the hole. Nothing happened. Finally, he knelt down and raked back the leaves so the skunk could be seen. The skunk did not move; it was dead. The farmer observed that the skunk was old, the teeth were broken, and concluded the skunk could no longer hunt for food and had prepared to die. Reading this story seemed foolish at the time, but God had a reason.

Seated about half way back in the coach section, a young soldier chose the empty seat beside me. As the plane took off, the soldier turned and said, "Sir, I probably won't be alive a year from now; I'm on my way to Vietnam." This matter of fact statement jolted my memory of the skunk story.

As the story was shared with the young soldier, his face became thoughtful. The time had come for me to present the claims of Christ. If an old skunk had enough sense to prepare to die, surely it would be wise for a soldier going to battle to make preparation to die.

The soldier's answer, "Sir, I would if I knew how." The door was wide open, and the ABC's of the gospel (All have sinned, Believe on the Lord Jesus Christ, and Confess with your mouth and you will be saved) were presented. The young soldier prayed to receive Christ and went to war prepared to die. God used spilled ink, an old newspaper, a plane ride, and a troubled, but searching heart, to do the work of redemption for a young soldier. I often thought about that young man. Perhaps I will see him again on the other side of Jordan.

121   MY GI HAIRCUT IN BANGKOK

During the Vietnam War, I had an opportunity as a USAF Reserve Chaplain (# 10078098) to go to Saigon to do some research for the Chaplaincy. I was interested in how the local churches in the States could augment the work of the military chaplain in the field. My Special Order T-20 came suddenly from Maxwell AFB, signed by Glenn H. Dowler, Lt.Col, USAF. To make my connection out of Travis AFB in California, I had to leave immediately. Dressed in my uniform, I rushed to the Atlanta airport planning to get a haircut. There was no time.

I sat by a young airman who cautiously said, "Sir, you better get a haircut." I explained my status and that I would get one at Travis AFB the next morning. There was no time. They were loading the planes for Vietnam. There was a seat for me. I boarded without a haircut. By now I was becoming self-conscious being surrounded by all the crew cuts of young men going to war. I received a few strange looks. I would point to my Chaplain's cross. The GI's would still look at me with disbelief, their eyes suggesting that even a Chaplain's cross does not excuse such a violation of the military code. I was beginning to wonder if even God could help me out of this situation.

The plane in front of us in the landing pattern received fire in an approach to Saigon. The pilot of my plane said, "Folks, I'm on pilots' discretion, and if you don't mind, I'm going to Bangkok!" At least now I could get a haircut.

Checking into my hotel, I located a barber shop. Since I was on a 30-day TDY assignment and would be back in my civilian clothes soon, I showed the barber with my fingers to take just a little off. You guessed it! He assumed I was on R&R and would be returning to the combat zone, so he gave me a first class GI haircut. I looked like Yul Brenner in The King and I. About 90 days later my hometown barber laughed as he shaved my neck and around my ears. He said, "I'll charge you for a shave not a haircut." As I get older and have only a few stray hairs on top, I often think of my GI haircut in Bangkok. Mostly, I remember how those young men with GI haircuts looked at me. I learned that a Call from God, Denominational Endorsement, and a Commission by the Chaplaincy did not relieve me of the basic rules that others must follow.

122   I HAD TIME TO KILL

While waiting in Bangkok, I tried to call my cousin, Col. Donald Curton, USAF, who commanded an air group in the Nha Trang area. I tried to call several times. He was my only relative in that part of the world. Because of the Tet offensive by the Viet Cong, all the phones were reserved for priority calls. A military operator would ask, "What is your priority code?" After several times, I spoke to a Sergeant and asked what kind of code do they want. He made up a code, something like, "Priority X4236JXQ." I used it, and the call went through to Nha Trang. "Col. Curton, Sir," was the answer. I said, "This is Hollis, and I . . ." I was interrupted with, "Hell, man, there's a war going on here!" followed by a noisy hang up.

It was two years before I learned the rest of the story. It seems that Donald was under his desk, under attack. His priority phone rang, and he thought it was a superior, perhaps giving him permission to pull out. I almost got him killed getting to the phone. Well, what good are kinfolk anyway, if you can't talk to them?

123   I NEVER REACHED SAIGON

Because of the Viet Cong Tet offensive, I never got to Saigon and was never able to complete my research for the Chaplaincy. I called my project officer from Bangkok and got permission to spend my TDY in the Philippines. I flew to Clark AFB and learned there was a religious retreat in the Baguio Mountains. It was a time of renewal and an opportunity to share with Christian servicemen. Other than the good fellowship, my most profound memory is of getting botulism from eating a pork chop at the home of a local missionary. It was an awful experience, but an Air Force Sergeant gave me a handful of little blue pills with instructions, "Sir, take them all at once." Those little blue pills put me back in the pink and stopped my extra trips to the facilities.

I often think of the young servicemen at the retreat who were returning to Vietnam and how precious life and health were when so many of us take it for granted. I never got to Saigon, but I did pray more earnestly for the young soldiers that were fighting and dying. After that experience I personally "signed" 500 Christmas cards each year and sent them addressed to the Combat Zone.

124   MY FAMILY'S WAR DEBT

From Travis AFB in California I made a quick call home before boarding the flight to Vietnam. My brother-in-law, George Stout, asked if I had a stopover in Manila, to pay a war debt for him. There was no time with all the research planned in Saigon, but I filed the idea in the back of my mind. When things went wrong in Saigon and I ended up in Bangkok and then on to the Philippines, I remembered my family's war debt.

I asked for permission to travel about 600 miles south of Manila to Zamboanga City and then on to Bascelian Island about 25 miles off the cost of Mindanao. The military said I must get permission from the Philippine government. They simply said, "No, it was too dangerous, because of the Moro tribe's uprising on Mindanao." The Moros were Muslim rebels and had never been conquered by anyone: not the Spanish, the English, the Dutch, the Americans, or the Japanese. They were particularly hostile to Christians and military personnel. The Philippine government said that an American Military Chaplain would be in great danger going into that area with the present state of civil unrest among the Moros.

When I told the government that I wanted to go and pay a family war debt, they changed their mind. They made me sign a waiver that they were not responsible for my safety and gave me about three hours of special briefing on how to conduct myself in the area. With all the papers signed, I put on civilian clothes and boarded an old Philippine plane. It was a rattle trap, or death trap, but we made it to Zamboanga City along with a few pigs and chickens. Inside the airplane looked like a rural bus loaded with a few people, but lots of animals.

The only way to reach Bascelian Island was by boat in the open sea about 25 miles in the Sulu Archipelago. I found the boat, purchased a ticket, and waited for it to leave. It held about twelve passengers, but there were only four of us aboard. I was told it would not leave until the boat was full of passengers. With limited time, I bought the balance of the tickets so we could depart. I think that was the reason for the wait. They wanted the American to buy the empty seats.

As we traveled the twenty-five miles of open sea, we passed a number of small outriggers. One had a small boy perched on a beam at the bow no larger than my hand. I commented to a passenger how dangerous it looked for a child to ride up there. I was told that the boy was spotting fish for his father and that if he were to fall into the water the father would not even extend a paddle to him. He would have to swim and catch up on his own. When I appeared shocked at such paternal disdain, the man responded, "He probably has four or five other sons at home; he would just bring another one on the next trip." Finally, we arrived on the Island.

At the dock I asked for directions to the home of Zoilo Melcompton. He was well known on the Island, and his home was easy to find. There were voices inside the house, so I knocked on the door. A middle-aged woman opened the door. I ask for Zoilo. A small man appeared and looked at me, surprised to see an American. When I said, "George Stout, sent me," the man screamed and slammed the door, and I heard him running up the stairs. Shocked, I slowly walked toward the steps assuming Zoilo didn't want anything to do with anyone who knew George. I was confused.

Hearing the door open, I turned to see Zoilo holding a large brown tube; I thought it was a bazooka. He saw the fear in my eyes and said, "For George, I make for George a map of Philippines." He unrolled the tube; it was a closely woven mat that included a map of the Philippines with the words "George Stout" at the bottom.

George had corresponded with him for several years, but Zoilo's most recent Christmas card to George was returned and marked, "No forwarding address." Zoilo didn't understand that George had moved, but thought George just didn't want to write anymore. He had planned to ship the straw mat/map to George for Christmas, but didn't have a working address. I agreed to take it back to America.

George Stout had told me how the Melcompton family had helped him during the war by hiding him under their floor from the Japanese. After V-J Day, George returned with a Navy Construction Battalion to rebuild the town buildings. The family had fed him, washed his clothes, and helped the Navy find Japanese soldiers who remained on the island after the surrender. George told me to buy them a washing machine and a refrigerator, but they did not have electricity. What was I to do to pay the war debt? I suggested that they go to town with me and I would buy them dinner. This we did, and everyone ate heartily.

The Melcomptons had a teenage daughter, so I decided to buy her a dress. There were no clothes for sale on the island, only broad cloth. The daughter picked out some cloth, and I bought enough for her mother to make her two dresses. The mother would not let me buy her any cloth.

She wanted the money. I gave her a twenty-dollar bill, and she disappeared.

She went straight to the street and bet it on a rooster fight and lost what was equal to a year's pay. Realizing that they did not know the worth of American money, I decided that my effort of the dinner and the cloth . . . plus the $20 was sufficient pay, under the circumstances. With the war debt settled, I went to the International Hotel to spend the evening.

The hotel was an old concrete block building constructed by the US Navy after World War II in an effort to assist the Island people. Several years of poor management and no repairs had left the hotel in terrible shape. The plumbing didn't work. There were no sheets on the bed, and the lock on the door was broken. I spread my plastic rain coat on the bed and put a shirt over the pillow and attempted to go to sleep.

The room was on the second floor just above the busy street. The people were gambling on rooster fights, drinking, dancing in the streets, and making lots of noise. I couldn't go to sleep for the noise and the condition of the room, but I decided to at least rest. Suddenly, everything went silent. I thought I had become deaf. I popped my fingers and could hear, but I couldn't explain the silence.

I had been told by the government about the Moro uprising and how they carried guns and took what they wanted. I had seen some on the streets carrying pistols in their belts. It looked like the Wild West in the movies. Are they coming to get me? Do they want my "stuff?" I was frightened; no, I was scared. It was a long night.

Before daylight I was on the dock waiting for the boat. There were a few civilized folk around. I met a couple of American college-aged men with the Peace Corps. Their

presence made me feel better. When the boat boarded, I
was glad to be heading for Zambonaga City and on to Manila.
The war debt was paid, but I was a casualty of a war of
nerves. I was also headed home and I thought of the young
men still in harms way.

125 AN ENGINE STOPPED OVER THE PACIFIC

Returning from my short excursion to Vietnam, Thailand,
and the Philippines on SAM (Space Available Military) flights,
I finally boarded a flying boxcar at Hicham AFB (Hawaii)
returning empty from Vietnam to March AFB (California).
It was noisy and cold. Beside the crew, there was a young
airman returning to get married. He was nervous and talked
a lot about everything. Finally, I climbed into the top bunk
in the rear crew's quarters, stuffed toilet paper in my ears,
and attempted to sleep.

About two hours into the flight over the Pacific, an alarm
sounded, the emergency lights came on in the empty cargo
area, and the crew began rushing around. Awakened by the
noise, I attempted to get up, but forgot I was on the top
bunk. I fell hard and let out a loud "Oh!" The young airman
in the lower bunk helped me to my feet and inquired about
my foot. Then, he rushed to the window overlooking the wing
and shouted the motor has stopped.

The pilot had shut the engine down because of an oil
leak. The crew was able to take a panel off the inside and
make the necessary repairs. The engine was soon running
again. The crew knew we were never in danger, but the
young airman and I didn't know the facts. Startled from
a dead sleep, naturally, we were "scared to death." We
took pictures of the stopped engine just to prove we were
there. Later the crew got a good laugh listening to the
airman talking about "floating in a rubber raft in the middle

of the Pacific, while his bride waited at the church." He was serious, but the way he carried on, it was hilarious. I had family waiting for me, too!

126 THE VANISHING VW IN RIO

Traveling in Brazil several years ago, I accompanied a local pastor in Rio de Janeiro on a visit to a member's home. He parked his VW bug on the street and entered to pray with a sick parishioner. We were there about fifteen minutes. When we returned, the VW was still there, but the engine and all four wheels were missing. The pastor's response, "It is part of the price of doing ministry in this community."

It would be helpful if the supporters of foreign missions and inter-city work in the USA clearly understood both the cost and the risk missionary pastors take on a daily basis. It would cause most to be more generous in their giving and more thankful in their prayers that God permitted them to stay at home and support others on the front lines of ministry.

127 TRANSLATION OFF, THE MEANING CLEAR

On a trip to Lima, Peru, with a group of missionaries, I was late arriving at the hotel the day we were to depart. Vessie Hargrave was in charge. He told the Doorman at the Hotel, "When Mr. Green comes, tell him we could not wait. He should saddle up his donkey and hurry to the airport." Given the message in Spanish, the Doorman clearly understood, but his English translation to me was a little off.

When I arrived about ten minutes after the group left for the airport, the Doorman rushed up to me and gave me a note. He had made a free translation in English: "Mr. Hargrave say, you put ass in the saddle and go airport quick." The translation was a little off, but the meaning was clear. I got a cab and made the flight. I shared the note with the group. Everyone had a good laugh. Cross-cultural communication is not easy.

128   "SIN" ALCOHOL

Taking a group of ministers and their wives on a South American trip, we arrived in Rio. I always stayed in a small hotel on Copacabana Beach where I was known. Since none on the trip spoke Portuguese, I arranged with the hotel to play a joke on my group. Brazil has a non-alcoholic drink known as "Guarana" that looks like champagne. The bottle clearly had a brand name Champagne, but is marked "sin alcohol." "Sin" in Portuguese means "without." Since none on the trip could read the language, my joke should work.

The group gathered, and I explained the local drink, "Guarana," that I wanted them to try. The waiter wrapped a towel around the magnum bottle and served everyone. They enjoyed the refreshing taste and asked for another round, so I took the opportunity to question the waiter about the "alcohol." He showed me the bottle; it clearly said "sin alcohol" which sounds bad to a group of English-speaking teetotalers. Sin alcohol sounded like the worst kind of alcohol.

I passed the bottle around so all could see the label on the bottle "Champagne Guarana--Sin Alcohol." They agreed it was an honest mistake and that no one should be upset . . . or tell anyone back home about it. Their clergy ordination had required them to vow to have nothing to do with alcohol… especially bad would be something in a foreign country labeled "sin alcohol!" My guests believed that "sin alcohol" was the worst kind. Later when they learned it was a joke, most were not pleased. They were still concerned that someone would tell the story and people would believe they were drinking "sin alcohol."

129   DON'T HANG PANTS ON THE BED POST

I was visiting Jamaica on a mission trip. The room where I slept did not have screens, and the windows were left open at the top for ventilation. Before retiring, the missionary instructed me to take my wallet, watch, and any other valuables and put them in the top drawer of the dresser. "Do not hang your pants with your stuff in them on the bed post." This was a strange request, since I wasn't in the habit of hanging my pants on the bed post. I pressed for an explanation.

Several things had been missing from their home. His explanation was that thieves would take a fishing pole and work through the open window during the night and "fish" valuables from the dresser or from pants hanging on the bed posts. He said, "They can hook your pants, pull them to the window, take all the valuables, and replace the pants without waking you."

I faithfully put my few valuables in the drawer and closed it good. I was tempted to hang my pants on the bed post, but thought better of the idea. It was a restless night. I didn't sleep much just thinking about someone "fishing" for my pants in my bedroom! With the window open at the top, the mosquitoes were bad, too. I burned a mosquito ring; it kept the bugs away long enough for me to go to sleep. As soon as the ring burned out, the mosquitoes came. Since mosquitoes love the white meat of a Southern boy, they kept me awake. While awake I kept watching for a fishing pole to come through the window "fishing" for my few valuables. In all, it was a bad night. Travel is not always fun.

130 I ATE MY FIRST LAMB IN LONDON

Preaching at Kensington Temple in the London area was a new experience. Aware of the cultural and language differences, I was careful in selecting my words. As I shared about the woman who had ten coins and lost one, I said, "She swept the floor..." The pastor said, "She brushed the floor..." I made a few more blunders, but none so foolish as my statement about eating my first lamb at Sunday lunch.

Lamb was not something one would normally find on the Green's table. I had never eaten lamb, and the green mint sauce, which was supposed to flavor the meat, just made it more difficult. Presentation and culture play a big role in the acceptance of food. I made an attempt to "taste" the lamb, but just could not eat it.

In the evening service I made a comment about lunch and said, "I ate my first lamb at lunch." When everyone laughed, I continued, "Not a whole lamb, just a taste." Now the audience was really amused. The image of the visiting speaker eating a whole lamb was more than they could politely handle. I think that was to be my first and last taste of lamb. I do remember that I was served some curried goat in Jamaica, but that certainly was not lamb. I didn't like the curried goat either.

131 THE HUMPED ZEBRA CROSSING

Since 1984, it has been my custom to take graduate students to the University of Oxford each January for research at the Bodleian Library. Walking from Wellington Square to the main building of Oxford University Press one rainy and foggy day, I was startled to see a sign, "Humped Zebra Crossing." I immediately conjured in my mind some prehistoric animal that look like a camel with Zebra stripes. It was a rare and humorous moment in Oxford.

The English call their speed bumps "Sleeping Policemen." An English crosswalk is painted black with white strips and is called a Zebra Crossing. When the crosswalk is intended to be a speed bump to slow vehicles, it is raised above the surface and becomes a Humped Zebra Crossing! This is what I had encountered on that rainy day.

Certainly I was confused, but it was a happy moment, and I tried to purchase such a sign for the Crystal Springs Campus of Oxford Graduate School in Tennessee. I attempted to purchase such a sign from the City of Oxford, but the cost to produce and ship such a metal sign to the USA was "beyond budget."

When I arrived in Tennessee, I asked an artist/sign maker to create such a sign. The anticipation of the consternation of visitors is exciting. Maybe such a sign would slow campus traffic just a bit as they conjure up a picture of a prehistoric camel with zebra stripes. It may be safer to cross Oxford Drive to the Study Centre or walk to The Gathering Place. Anyway, that was my plan, but when the signs arrived the camel was a donkey with a hump on his back. I was disappointed, but in fairness the sign maker had never seen a Humped Zebra. The signs were never posted.

132 WHY DID GOD PUT US TOGETHER?

On the Oxford Graduate School campus you will find a plaque and a Study Centre honoring William O. Green, my uncle, who when he heard that Hollis was starting a school, wrote a sizeable check and said, "I want to give the first offering to encourage Hollis in this ministry." There is another plaque on the Tower Court of the chapel to Noah Davis and his wife that reads, "They first trusted the vision!" The Davis' provided a no interest loan for 10 years to assist with the opening of the academic program. Many who provided the "seed money" for the early development of the educational program have passed to their reward, but their legacy remains. It is still providing a quality graduate education to each student who enters the Oxford campus.

Please note the Scripture that makes clear that those who are the first to give have "understood the Lord's thoughts." Thank God for the First Givers. This honor roll will continue as others understand the Lord's thoughts and join to support the academic ventures.

There is a fathomless depth in God's wisdom and knowledge! His judgments are unsearchable, and His footsteps cannot be tracked! Who can figure out the mind of the Lord? Or who could be His advisor? Who has first given to God that He should pay back again? For God is the source, preserver, and ruler of all things: to God is glory throughout all ages. Amen. (Romans 11:33-36 DNT)

We must also remember the early Oxford leaders who gave unselfishly of their time and energy: MGen Curry, Chairman Sullivan, Dr. Irvin, Dr. Patterson, Dr. Liebig, Professors Swanson, Jackson, Morgan, Finigan, Humphrey, Faust, Kittell, Pix, Mould, Justice, Standridge, and VanBroekhoven. These sacrificed to assure that students during the early decades were properly prepared to become "World Changers."

My standard response when an individual is brought into my path by chance is to ask, "Why did God put us together? Am I supposed to do something for you? Are you supposed to help me with something? Or perhaps, God intends us to do something together." There are two additional incidents that bear on the developing days of my academic initiatives: (1) the OXFORD GRADUATE SCHOOL program in the USA, and (2) the establishment of OASIS UNIVERSITY in Trinidad, W.I.

(1) In 1985 I boarded a plane for Washington, D.C.; the only seat left was by a well-dressed lawyer looking gentleman. After take-off, I turned to the gentleman and introduced myself and asked, "Did God put you here to help me, am I supposed to assist you with something, or does God intend us to do something together?" Usually, the people just look at me as if I am crazy, but if the meeting is truly of God it is a good way to find out quickly. In this case, it was providential.

The gentleman's name was David Lemons from Florida, and he wanted to know exactly what I was doing. When he understood that I was initiating a new graduate school program, he immediately said, "Then you need library books." He gave me clear directions that I followed step by step and produced library books valued over one million dollars. These volumes are housed on campus in the Oxford Library Reserve.

(2) In November of 2001, Gail and I went to Trinidad to preach and recruit. In a TEAM OXFORD meeting 32 prospects came for lunch, but only two were willing to come to the USA to study. After the meeting Steve Mohammed and a man named "Subesh Ramjattan" came to see me at the hotel. Following a discussion about the Oxford program with Steve, I turned to Subesh and asked, "Did God send you here to help me, am I supposed to help you, or can we do something together?" Subesh responded, "I sold my business in the US and put the funds in trust for Trinidad. I am building a compound above the University, come see if you can use it?" This conversation resulted in OASIS UNIVERSITY (Omega Advance Schools for Interdisciplinary Studies) that is serving the Caribbean with a global vision.

Christians should never ignore the people whom God places in their path. With respect to the Sovereignty of God, each one of us must have the courage to engage each contact until we fully understand the reason God placed them in our path.

Please understand not every person one meets is sent from God. There is another power involved in the affairs of men, known as the Evil One or Satan. On a case by case basis, one must test "the spirits to see if they are of God." Then move forward with confidence. This is how God's work is accomplished in the world.

133 A TRUCKER'S FRIDAY POEM

My work has always required me to travel. One meets all kinds of people. And they are not all born again believers washed in the blood and singing glory, glory... At times one gets bored just listening to the radio. In those days the CB was a good thing to keep one awake at night. Traveling in New York State, my wife and I were shocked to hear on the CB, "It's time for my Friday poem:

> God made man; He made him out of strang, He had a little left, so he made a little thang.

> God made woman, He made her out of lace, He didn't have enough, so He left a little place.

Then a trucker was heard to respond, 'THANK GO-D-D-D!'"

Following closely was a voice that said, "Hey, trucker you ought to be ashamed to talk like that on the CB. Others beside truckers are listening." To this the trucker responded, "This CB channel 19 is for truckers, if you don't like the language, turn to another channel." I guess that is the answer, if who we meet or hear is not in keeping with our values, we just change the channel. Somewhere out there is a clear voice that will please God and advance His cause. As we travel, we must be selective. By chance God gives us the opportunity to choose. Choosing channels and talking with selected people is a good thing!

134   A SHRINE IN PERU

Traveling in Peru gathering stories for a magazine, I arrived in Lima on the week the Pope declared several saints were to be taken off the official Vatican list. I searched the streets of Lima seeking someone who could speak English better than I could speak Spanish. Finally, I found a young man about 25 and asked him about the Pope's decision to take certain saints off the list. He said it didn't matter, that the people could still pray to them, but the church just wouldn't teach the next generation to recognize them. I asked, "Why would you want to continue to pray to a saint the Pope says is really not worthy?"

The young man responded in effect that the idea of saints was to encourage people to pray; the power was not in the saint, but in the person praying. That was good reasoning, so I pushed the conversation, "What is a saint, and why does the Church select them?" He proceeded to explain that a saint was someone who lived so good and holy that they bypassed Purgatory and went straight to Heaven when they died.

According to his definition and my theology, since I did not accept the concept of purgatory, I was a Saint. I stuck out my hand and said, "I am Saint Hollis!" He appeared frightened, but did not say a word. He just turned and walked away rapidly. After a few steps, he turned and took another look at me, a few more steps, and turned again. I think he believed that I was one of the saints that had been taken off the list who had appeared to him. I observed as he continued toward the Church just down the block where I assumed he would pray or tell his Priest about Saint Hollis.

I have not returned to Lima since that date, but if I were to travel to Lima again I certainly would take a look on that corner to see if there is a shrine to Saint Hollis. Whether they built a shrine to me or not, sometimes I feel kind of "saintly." My sons say I feel saintly because I am getting old, losing my hair, and my beard has turned white.

If I am not seen as a "saint", perhaps I have become a "sage". A sage is someone who is regarded as knowledgeable, wise, and experienced, especially a man of advanced years revered for his wisdom and good judgment. Perhaps I am both, a saint for my religious faith and a sage for my academic adventures. Either way I am satisfied with myself. I do hope they built a shrine to "Saint Hollis" in Lima. I am certain that one fellow will remember me, for sure!

135 GOAL WAS TO KILL TEN ISRAELIS

Flying out of Rio de Janeiro, Brazil, my seat mate was a young Arab graduate student. Not often does a Protestant clergyman get to talk for an extended period with an intellectual from Syria. I looked forward to a learning experience, because I always appreciated a cross-cultural conversation. A few minutes into the flight, I decided to engage the young man in conversation. "What are your goals in life?" I asked quietly.

"I have but one goal. My life would be completely fulfilled if I could kill ten Israelis!" was his terse reply. He continued, "I would be willing to give my life in the process of completing that goal."

I wondered how many young Christian students would be willing to give their lives in an advancement of the Cause of Christ. I could not think of a single person that I truly believed was willing to die for their Christian convictions. That was a tragic conclusion. There was little left to talk about. We both read most of the trip. If the door is not open or is closed in your face, don't try to walk where angels fear to tread.

136 NO CHALLENGE IN CHRISTIANITY

A friend of mine, Lewis J. Willis, sat by Muhammad Ali on a flight out of Atlanta soon after the boxer converted to Islam and changed his name. Mr. Willis asked him why he made the switch from Christianity to Islam. The response was shocking.

"There was no challenge in Christianity; Islam gave me a way to change the world." Ali was confident in his statement, firm in his conviction, and satisfied with his decision. Who failed Cassias Clay? Did someone fail to lead him to a personal experience with Christ? Who missed an opportunity to harness this strong voice as a Christian witness?

I firmly believe the Christian faith provides a means to change individuals and the world. True conversion works. Anything less is not valid Christianity. True believers can change the world one person and one day at a time. The big question, "How many others will we let slip through the cracks and become a spokesperson for another religion?" Christianity must compete for the souls and hearts of the young in the marketplace to remain viable. What have you done today to advance the Cause of Christ? In your travels don't miss the opportunity to witness to God's saving grace. I believe that "Opportunity equals obligation."

137 GOD'S ADVERBS

Traveling alone down Interstate 75 south of Atlanta, the long journey ahead suggested a hitch hiker might be good company. As the young man entered the car, "Good morning,

my name is Hollis Green; I am a Christian." The response
was "Carl Krudof, I am a philosopher." The young philosopher
was baited, "Do you write your philosophy down, or do you
just talk?" He claimed to write important thoughts down.
He was asked about his most recent writings.

Carl said, "I have just written a definition of God, but I
don't believe there is one."

[A definition of God by a philosopher who doesn't believe
in God. This was going to be interesting.]

Reaching into the back seat to retrieve a small unzipped
notebook, Carl began to read: "God is the singular,
possessive, abstraction of the adverb."

[He is a philosopher; my teachers talked that way. Carl
was asked to repeat the first statement.]

He repeated, "God is the singular, possessive, abstraction
of the adverb."

[What's an adverb? I've been out of school too long.]

Carl continued, "An adverb is the linguistic manifestation of
a life process."

It is my conviction that God provides both the situation
and the supplies to share with others the good news. The
discussion centered on Carl's definition. It was good theology
for a philosopher who did not believe. This was discussed
at length. His use of the present tense initiated a long
exchange. The singularity of one God was discussed. The
possessive nature of God was considered. God's ways being
past finding out are kind of an abstraction.

Somewhere in Carl's intellectual's comprehension, the use
and function of the adverb was the key to an adequate
perception of God. "An adverb is the linguistic manifestation
of a life process." God was not viable to Carl because there
was no systematic order relating the signs and symbols

about a Divine Person to his personal reality. God in this case was the big Noun, and Carl had never witnessed the action of God in real time. He needed someone who had personally experienced the power and action of God to adjust the semantics and syntax of the experience to a language he could accept. Carl needed the same touch of experiential reality that Thomas of scripture desired. Carl needed a touch of first hand personal reality. He required a manifestation of the resurrected life of Jesus Christ. At last, the course of action was clear. Carl needed to see one of God's adverbs.

This called for a new introduction, "Good morning, my name is Hollis Green; I am one of God's adverbs." A spark of cognition ignited; Carl's mind was open; the heart was ready; and the Holy Spirit had done His work. A simple walk down the Roman Road of scripture brought Carl face to face with the reality of the man Christ Jesus. He accepted not only the present tense existence of the Creator, but a personal relationship with Jesus, the Son. Carl was greeted as a Brother, a fellow adverb to go forth and point to the real time action of God.

What the world needs is more of God's Adverbs sharing the excitement of living the Christian life. Are you willing to be one of God's Adverbs ready to magnify and point to the blessings of God that are available to all who believe? If so, blessings are on the way. It is always a joy to share the testimony of grace to someone who is reaching for divine assistance.

138   I DON'T WANT TO BE SAVED

Each January near my birthday, a personal effort is made to pray, plan, and think about the coming year. What can be done differently? What can be done better? What can be done new that would advance the gospel? Living in Atlanta during my time of meditation, I was impressed to travel to New York City. Using a credit card, I traveled to LaGuardia. A ride to the hotel, a good night's sleep, and then perhaps understanding would come as to why God impressed me to travel to NYC.

In bed, almost asleep, the phone rang. The front desk clerk spoke clearly, "Dr. Green, please come to the Lobby." Past ministry had placed me in 17 different churches in NYC, but no one knew my present plans. Putting my pants over my PJ's, the only thought was to follow the directions to the lobby.

As the elevator door opened, a man dressed only in pants, no shirt or shoes, was holding a wrecking bar in one hand and a pair of scissors in the other. He turned and saw me, "I don't want to be saved," he screamed. At that moment my mission was clear.

Walking up to the man with an outstretched hand, he gave me his weapons and answered the question about his room number. About this time the NY Police came in to make an arrest, but the explanation that the hotel had asked me to handle the situation caused the officer to delay. Agreeing that it was bad whiskey and that a night's sleep could change things for him, the police agreed to put a guard outside his door. The troubled man went to sleep.

Returning to my room, my heart was pounding. Questions filled my head. My phone rang again; it was the man. "Are you the gentleman who helped me downstairs?" With an affirmative answer, he asked for my prayers. Scheduling a wake-up call at 6:30 AM, and a planned meeting in the coffee shop at 7:15 AM, sleep finally came.

The next morning in the coffee shop, with my New Testament in hand, the man was asked a simple question:

"Do you believe this book is the Word of God?" He was unsure, and on follow-up, said he did not know anyone who believed the Bible. Then, as if out of the clear blue, he said, "An old man in Boston a few weeks ago talked with me about being born again. He believed the Bible! Do you think that born again business would help me?"

The door was open; God was working. A simple explanation about believing with the heart and confessing with the mouth was sufficient. It was not a scheduled church activity; it was a personal witness in the marketplace that God used to change this life. A letter confirming that change came a few days later on a Washington, D.C., letterhead. God does work in mysterious ways to perform His work in the world. It is always good to be included in the action. God is not interested in our abilities; He wants our availability.

139   CROWN ROOM BECAME A SANCTUARY

Traveling opens many doors for the gospel. The real challenge for the church is in the marketplace, out where the people are on a daily basis. At a NY airport waiting in line for a delayed night flight, two gentlemen were in line talking around me. When they would not break line, their conversation was forced on me.

Understanding their frustration, my Delta Flying Colonel Card was used to take them to a more private place to wait. The Crown Room was almost deserted. Soft drinks were in the refrigerator and little fish crackers on the counter, so the munching started.

After a while, one asked, "Do you work for the airline?" A negative answer was not sufficient; the follow-up question dealt with my occupation. They were told about my travels, writing, and speaking. One asked, "What do you write?" Sharing with them about discipleship, evangelism, and dying churches in America, one said, "My church is spiritually dead, and I am too!" With this the other one decided to leave. Alone, God worked the mysterious process of renewal and commitment.

A note on Delta stationary from the Crown Room arrived in the mail. It listed "7 Things God Did For Me Today." Religion is not dead, and the cause of Christ is alive and well; it is just functioning better on an individual basis than it is at the organized level.

140 THE MESSAGE OF THE TICKET

Teaching in seminary, I constantly reminded the class of future preachers that they were not "called to ministry" unless they loved dogs, kids, and old folks. They were told they could never fool anyone about the true nature of their feelings. Even a stray dog would know whether or not they were loved. So do the children and most certainly the old folks.

About to return from Tennessee to my home in Florida, I told my elderly mother to come visit me. She said, "You don't want me to come!" Shocked and even hurt, I protested, "You are my mother, of course, I want you to visit my home." Mother responded, "I'm an old woman on Social Security. If you wanted me to come you would give me a ticket!" You just can't fool the old folks. I bought her an open ticket and renewed my invitation to "Come visit us whenever you wish." She came; in fact, she almost beat us to Florida.

Preaching a series of services in New Jersey, I shared this story about Mother and the ticket. As the meeting closed, the pastor asked if the people wanted me to return. One Brother responded, "Give that man a ticket!" Actions do speak louder than words. Do you know someone who needs a ticket?

141　EVERYONE NEEDS HELP

I was scheduled to speak to a leadership group at the Rolls Royce plant in Derby, UK the week the Super Sonic Transport, SST Project went bankrupt. Rolls Royce made the engines, and Lockheed was constructing the air frame. Both went under, and the US government had to bail out Lockheed while the UK government had to assist Rolls Royce.

After my address, I was given a tour of the plant making the Super Sonic Transport engines. They were large; several men could be seen working inside the large motor. There were small fan blades on the front of the engine. I asked the guide if I could have one. "Why do you want a piece of this engine?" I said, "If big companies such as Rolls Royce and Lockheed need help, we all need help. I want to make a plaque and place a piece of this engine on it and call attention to the fact that 'EVERYBODY NEEDS HELP."

He told me all parts were classified, protected by heavy security, numbered, and must be accounted for each shift. Broken pieces must be melted down and the material reused. It is a special material. The next morning in my hotel box was a small plain brown envelope filled with cotton. Inside the cotton was a small fan blade. I made the plaque. It reminds me that we all need help now and then and should never be reluctant to ask for support from those able to provide assistance.

142　WATER, WHATEVER FOR, SIR?

In January, 1984, I took a group of graduate students to the University of Oxford for research. The group stayed at the Royal Oxford Hotel on Park End Street. Americans are accustomed to drinking water with their meals. At the first evening meal, a student asked the waiter for a glass of water. "Water, Sir, whatever for?" The answer "To drink" surprised the Waiter. The Englishman responded, "We wash in water, but we don't drink it."

As the waiter walked away, presumably to get the glass of water, the American called, "Just bring a pitcher of water for the table!" The Englishman returned, "You want a picture of water for the table?" Finally, understanding what was requested, the waiter brought a container of water to the table and said, "This is a flask!"

143 SEPARATED BY A COMMON LANGUAGE

It has been said that America and England are two countries separated by a common language. This common language makes visitors feel less like a foreigner. One year, we invited an academic (Geoffrey Thomas, Ph.D.) from the University of Oxford to speak at the Oxford Commencement in Tennessee. He shared with the class an example of the problem with the language.

It seems that when an Englishman says "momentarily" he means "for a moment," but when an American uses the word "momentarily" he means "in a moment." Dr. Thomas asked, "Can you imagine how I felt when the American pilot said we will be taking off momentarily? I thought we will go up and immediately back down!" After this we provided students a dictionary of terms when they traveled to Oxford, UK. For example:

An elevator is a lift.

A truck is a lorry.

A single home is a detached house.

A duplex is a semi-detached house.

An apartment is a flat.

A car's trunk is a boot.

A car's hood is a bonnet.

The windshield is a windscreen.

Gasoline is called petrol.

A cookie is a biscuit.

A paper plate is a cardboard plate.

A drugstore is a Chemist.

You don't mail a letter, you post it.

A library card is a ticket.

You don't rent a car, you hire a car.

The highway is a motorway.

A 4-lane is a dual carriage-way.

UK drives on the correct side not the right side.

Personal weight is measured in stones.

And the list goes on...

144 WHO IS THE BEST LOOKING MAN?

The first year Mother accompanied the graduate school group to Oxford, England, the students were all male. Knowing Mother was a widow, the students teased her about coming on the trip looking for a husband. One evening at dinner Mother was asked, "Who is the best looking man on this trip?" Without hesitation Mother responded, "Donald Elliott!"

Quickly, I asked the person not to ask her for the other side of the coin. Mother was frank about everything. When you asked her a question she felt she must tell the truth. Through the years, Mother always asked me about Donald Elliott. I guess some people just make a good impression!

145 THE PROBLEM OF SCIENTIFIC LITERACY

A friend, G. P. Thomas, Ph.D., was lecturing to a group of American graduate students on scientific literacy at the University of Oxford. During the interaction, he shared with the class that the English had trouble understanding that the earth rotated on its axis rather that the sun actually rising and setting. A student aware of the dismal weather in England asked, "Sir, could it be that they have never seen the sun?" With scholarly contemplation Dr. Thomas answered, "Could be."

Could it be that cloudy weather causes some to doubt Holy Scripture, or are some confused by academic or scientific language? I guess it is all in perception. Does the sun appear to rise and set? Of course, it looks that way! Can we see the rotation of the earth? Surely, not! Some like Thomas must "see" while others believe even when they can't clearly see. It is called faith!

When scripture and science disagree, it is normally one of perception. Often when science disagrees with scripture, science is dealing with probability based on observation. There was a time when a Greek academic said there were only 4,000 stars in the sky. The natural eye could count 4,000 stars on the Greek hillside on a clear night. Later someone built a telescope and discovered many thousands more stars. Then NASA sent a telescope into space and man could see not only millions of stars, but also more galaxies. When science was "guessing," scripture told us that the "number of stars could not be counted." If science and scripture do not agree, just wait because science will catch up.

Remember the Russian space traveler who said he didn't see God. Well the truth is that God is "a Spirit" and is available to mankind only through faith's eye. "Jesus said to Thomas, because you have seen Me, you believed: blessed are they that have not seen, and yet have believed" (John 20:29 DNT).

146 TRAVELERS SHOULD SHARE GOOD NEWS

Some years ago traveling by train from London to Birmingham, England, many sheep were along the track. My knowledge of sheep was limited to the facts in the Bible. The only thing known was that sheep needed a shepherd. Seeing many sheep but no shepherds, an English traveling companion was asked, "Are the shepherds on strike?" The answer was firm and clear: "We don't have shepherds; we have fences." My understanding of sheep was expanded. Sheep must have either a shepherd or a fence, and sometimes both are needed.

Metaphors about sheep and shepherding were used to illustrate the shortcomings of people in scripture. Leaders were called good and bad shepherds. "All we like sheep have gone astray" is a well known phrase. Peter was told by Jesus, "Feed My sheep!" Around the world, we must be aware that the "sheep" need feeding and that God has equipped believers with the bread and fruit needed by a hungry world. With the mixed messages of the modern media, people are in dire need of good news. As we travel, the good news must be shared at every opportunity.

147 A KIND GESTURE MADE A FRIEND

Growing up in Chattanooga, Tennessee, I never considered the problem of race. My schools were segregated, but it was natural for that period of American history. It was just accepted. My paternal Grandfather, however, had taught me not to discriminate against people on the basis of color, but to use character, personality, and Christian unity as criteria for acceptance. Grandfather would use his hand to demonstrate what he meant. "Just like the open hand, people are separated on social issues, but like the closed fist, the people are together when evil is resisted." This was good guidance for me before Civil Rights came along.

As a teenager, I lived on the edge of the Black community and associated freely with young people of my own age. I didn't understand why we didn't attend the same school, but Mother explained that the City Fathers made rules and drew districts and that the district line ran down the middle of our street. It would have been good if such people had stayed the (expletive deleted) out of the good community relationships that the children had developed. Remember, prejudice has to be taught. Children are not born with such feelings.

During high school I worked on Friday evening and Saturday at a grocery store across the city. One Friday evening I began walking home because I didn't have bus fare. It was a long walk of several miles, but my friend, Willie Wise, drove by and picked me up. "Why are you walking, man? This is a bad part of town!" Realizing that I would rather ride, he let me out near my home and handed me bus fare to ride the bus to work the next morning. Now that's a good friend.

That kind gesture confirmed Willie as my best friend. He was older and had been in the Army. Life had not been easy for him; he was black. He recognized the need of a poor friend. Willie was what my Grandfather called a "giver." The world would be a better place if there were more wise men like Willie Wise! I learned that color didn't matter; it was character that counted.

148 CONSCIOUS OF THE PROBLEM OF RACE

My experience with Willie Wise made me more conscious of the problem of race. At every opportunity, I began to express my feelings about segregation. At the University of Cincinnati, a professor put me on the debate side against segregation since I was from the south. I won the debate with the argument that black people were only discriminated against when they sat down. They could stand in line, order food, buy stuff, even stand on the bus up front, but if they sat down everybody else stood up and hollered.

My solution was to put stand up desks in the schools, take all the seats out of public transportation and make everyone stand, and take the benches out of public parks and churches. I used the idea from the Bible that the rulers sat in the gates of the cities; the king had a throne. I talked about the seat of authority, such as a seat on the Supreme Court. Jesus stood up to read in the temple because the authority was in the Word not in the man. Somehow I convinced the audience that discrimination was based on an attempt to keep people of color out of positions of authority and that it was more political and cultural than it was racial.

My efforts were noticed by Dr. Martin Luther King, Jr. Just before Dr. King died he composed a list of 200 men most interested in Civil Rights in the South. My name appeared on that list. It has been a source of pride for me through the years.

149 EQUAL OPPORTUNITY AND THE PENTAGON

When Ronald Reagan was elected President I was considered for the Equal Opportunity position at the Pentagon. The actual position was Deputy Assistant Secretary of State for Equal Opportunity and was responsible for protecting minorities, both military and civilian, in relation to the Armed Forces. At that time about 18 million people were under the Equal Opportunity provisions of the Pentagon. Maj. Gen. Jerry R. Curry, USA, was my primary sponsor, but Bill Brock had cleared me politically with the White House. With these things in order, I went to Washington and was interviewed by Nofzinger and shown an office at the Pentagon and introduced to several high ranking military officers who worked in the E.O. Office.

Mr. Nofzinger asked me a straight question, "Dr. Green, being a member of the cloth, could you enforce the provisions of Equal Opportunity?" My answer was direct and honest, "I actually don't know. For many years I have encouraged people to associate freely along the basic concepts of equal opportunity. I honestly don't know how I would handle the 'authority' to force people to comply." With this bit of self-disclosure, I began to revise my interest in the position and told Mr. Nofzinger that I didn't want the position. I was going to Tennessee to start a graduate school.

I wrote a paper for President Reagan affirming that "Only the Majority can Protect the Minority." I explained that when a woman had the Pentagon position, she assisted blacks and Hispanics, but was unable to do much for women. The same was true when a black or Hispanic held the position. They assisted others, but were unable to facilitate the advancement of their own minority. I called for the elimination of all lower offices of E.O. in the Pentagon and asked that the authority and responsibility/accountability for E.O. remain at the highest offices where there was power and resources to actually do something. The lower E.O. offices could only agitate and litigate and probably cause more harm than good.

Surprisingly, my ideas were worthy, and many positions, including the one considered for me, were abolished. Equal

Rights made good progress when those in authority were held accountable rather that passing the buck to some underling where little was ever accomplished. So I moved to Tennessee and laid the foundation stones of Oxford Graduate School.

150   WHITE KNUCKLE SCARED

Viola Edgeman, a friend of my mother, accompanied us to England. She had never flown and was afraid to fly. Mother talked her into going, but she was still nervous about the actual flying part. I promised her that I would keep her informed and let her know what was happening so she would have no need to be afraid. When we boarded the plane, I explained that the aircraft would taxi out to a runway, run the engines up, and test all the dials and gauges. There would be lots of noise and movement of the plane. She shouldn't worry; I would tell her when we were about to take off so she could get white knuckle scared for sure.

We had been in the air about fifteen minutes when Viola asked, "Are we about ready to take off? It has been a long time." She was surprised to learn that we had been airborne for fifteen minutes. She commented, "What was there to be afraid of? I didn't even know when we took off!" I explained about the landing. The air would be rough the closer we got to the ground, there would be lots of noise when the landing gear was lowered, and there would be changes in the plane as the flaps were engaged. It was much the same story as the pre-flight presentation. She was told that I would tell her when we were about to land.

Over the coast of England there was lots of clouds and fog. Visibility was almost zero. The pilot made an instrument landing, but the fog was so thick you couldn't see the ground. As we rolled to a stop, Viola felt the movement, but she couldn't see the ground. "Are we about to land?"

When she learned that we had been on the ground about ten minutes, again she was surprised. Finally, she came to the conclusion that there was nothing to worry about. She relaxed and enjoyed her stay in England. The return flight to Atlanta was no problem; Viola was now a veteran traveler!

151   MOTHER'S TOMBSTONE MONEY

Mother made four trips to Oxford, England, with me and my student group. The third time she used her burying money to go, with the hope that she could save enough before she died to replace it. She did and prepaid her funeral.

Knowing she was getting old and the time would come when she could not travel overseas, I encouraged Mother to make one more trip with us. She just didn't have the money. My wife and I decided to pay her way. She would have nothing to do with us paying her way. I had to work a different strategy.

I took Mother to the grave site of my father and told her that when she died I was going to remove the small stone and replace it with a large stone that would have both her and Father's data on it. She said, "How much will this cost?" The numbers I gave her were way too rich for her blood. "No," she said, "Just put a small stone for me and save your money." "In that case," I told her, "I could afford to take the money I was going to spend on the tombstone and pay your way to England." To this she agreed.

In England, some of the students asked if she was rich making so many overseas trips. Mother responded, "I'm certainly not rich. I used my tombstone money to make this trip."

152   A NEW CHRISTIAN'S FAITH

Dr. Steve Gyland was a Pediatrician in Florida. He and Rose, his wife, attended my evening seminary class one semester. During a break, I overheard Steve talking with another student about the things for which he had prayed that week. He had plumbing problems at his office and a roof leak at home. He had prayed and asked God to fix these problems. Deciding that this young Christian needed some counseling, I suggested to him that God was not a plumber or a roofer and that one should not bother God with things they were well able to fix themselves.

The respectful response of this medical doctor put me in my place. He said, "Dr. Green, it doesn't diminish God a bit to do little things for me. I know I am kind of childish, but let me enjoy my new faith." Then he added, "Someday I guess I'll become a mature Christian and start bearing burdens like you." Out of the mouths of "Baby Believers" will the clergy be instructed. God has a simple plan: "Except you become as a little child, you will not enter the kingdom of Heaven." Perhaps we should listen more to new converts.

153   A TRAIN TRIP TO WASHINGTON, D.C.

Steve Gyland, MD, (Pediatrician) asked Gail and me to travel with him and others by train to participate in the Washington for Jesus Parade. The train was crowded. There was lots of talking and singing. No one could sleep. Arriving tired and sleepy, we had to hurry to get organized for our part in the parade. Dr. Gyland was in charge of the Florida group and was supposed to police who marched. The organizers had provided information to the group leaders about the possibility of certain groups crashing the parade.

The group was organized, and the parade began. About half way through, a group called "Children of God" dressed in white cloth with ropes for belts abruptly joined the march. They used cloth and rope, but no leather. As a small gap developed between the Florida group and the one in front, about a dozen of the Children of God jumped into the parade. Marching in front of us, Dr. Gyland became concerned about this unauthorized group. He turned and asked, "Does anyone have a Bible?"

No one seemed to have one, but Gail had a New Testament in her purse. She handed it to Dr. Gyland. Steve opened the Testament and holding it in his left hand with the pages facing forward, he raised his right hand and prayed silently. No words were spoken to the intruders, but Dr. Gyland walked behind each one and held the open Testament behind their head. One by one they turned and sat down on the curb. It was the most mysterious and powerful silent prayer and demonstration of faith I ever witnessed.

Most members of the group saw the event and were astounded by the power of simple faith. It would be marvelous if all converts to the Christian faith could keep that "first generation" faith active in their lives. BUT, who would carry all the heavy burdens and worry? You see, worry is taking responsibility for something that belongs to God. So who is going to do the worrying?

154   A PRAYING GENERAL

Maj. Gen. Jerry R. Curry, USA, called my home one Friday evening from the airport. "I sense that there is a fire brewing at the school." His many years of combat experiences had developed a keen sense of intuition. On one occasion in Korea, Curry's troops were surrounded with little hope of breaking out or for reinforcements fighting their way

in to save them. He sent a radio message for the artillery
to blast a hole in the enemy circle at a given time. "Where
do you want the bombardment?" Thinking the enemy might
be listening, Curry told the man to remember the "Star of
Bethlehem." The bombardment came in the East on time,
and Curry's troops escaped the trap.

Remembering this story about Korea, I rushed back to
school. Monday was to be a holiday. The school would be
closed from Friday afternoon until Tuesday morning. When
I arrived at the school, I found three possible fire hazards.
Someone had put pennies behind the fuses in an old section
of a building; the box was so hot I could hardly touch it to
turn off the main. A secretary had left an electric heater
on under her desk next to an overflowing waste basket filled
with paper. A bathroom door had been propped open against
a wall heater. The paint on the door was already peeling. I
learned to trust experience and intuition, especially from a
praying General who believed in the present ministry and work
of the Holy Spirit.

155 I HAVE GROWN SINCE LAST YEAR

One of my students in a Washington, D.C., seminar was
Maj. Gen. Jerry R. Curry, USA. Although he was a man
of great authority and experience, he was an excellent
student. To have such a distinguished military man in the
class was a source of encouragement for me. Gen. Curry
was transferred to Colorado Springs and some months later
attended my seminar in Denver. At the afternoon break, I
shared with him that the last two hours of the class would
cover some material from the D.C. seminar the year before.
He was told he could be excused if he needed to return to
base. He was direct and clear, "Sir, I will stay. I have
grown since last year. I will hear it differently!"

Gen. Curry stayed and took more notes. After class he showed me his notes. There was a line down the middle of the page with the previous notes on the left and the new notes on the right side. There were several entries. He had truly heard different things. One could clearly see how a poor, teenage, minority enlistee from Philadelphia had become a two star general.

156   DON'T FIX WHAT AIN'T BROKE

Most of us continually revisit the same work in an effort to make things better. Constant meddling often causes one to attempt to fix something that doesn't need fixing. The effort is wasted, and other things that need to be done are left unfinished. The tragedy is that sometimes in attempting to make things better we actually make the matter worse. Maj. Gen. Jerry R. Curry, USA, in 1981 became the founding Chair of the Board of Regents for Oxford Graduate School.

In the early days of the school, Gen. Curry would remind the faculty and staff that there was too much good to be done to work on things that didn't need fixing. Reminding us of his aggressive leadership philosophy, he would repeat, "Don't fix what ain't broke!" We concentrated on things that needed fixing, and there is a viable institution today as a result.

157   WINTER TIME AT CHRIST CHURCH

On an early trip to Oxford, England, I invited my mother to accompany the faculty and students. She loved to travel and enjoyed the trip so much, she returned three additional times to England. On the first trip, we went to Evensong at Christ Church, Oxford. It was January, and the weather

was cold. There was little central heat, and everyone
wore coats, gloves, scarves, and the women's hats covered
their ears. During the service, the program required the
congregation to stand, bow, kneel, pray, stand, bow, kneel,
pray -- it seemed continuous.

Walking back to the Royal Oxford Hotel, Mother turned to
me and said, "So that's where all that standing and kneeling
in church came from . . . they had to do that to keep the
congregation from freezing to death!" Without the process
one would get mighty cold in most English churches during
winter services.

A few years later George Finigan and I joined Charles
Mould, then Secretary of the Bodleian Library, for a morning
service in an old stone church at Shipton on Wychwood.
When we arrived, the foggy breath coming from each member
seated in the congregation caused George to whisper to
me, "Everyone is smoking to stay warm." It was cold, but
the fellowship and the worship were warm. It was a joy to
worship with friends in a place that had been used to honor
God for so many generations. Adrienne, Dr. Mould's wife, is
buried there now. I look forward to visiting the old church
again and the grave of my friend. Meanwhile, I have planted
a tree on the campus to honor Charles and Adrienne and
their interest in Oxford Graduate School at Crystal Springs.
Their friendship through the years has made the journey
worthwhile.

158   THE SPOON STOOD IN THE CUP

On one of the annual trips to Oxford, England, Ted Gee,
a student, brought along some powdered coffee creamer for
personal use. At each meal, someone would ask Ted for a
little creamer for their coffee. The response was always the
same, "I have just enough for me, sorry."

Ted had pulled some pranks on members of the group, which prompted drastic action. Securing some clear, unflavored gelatin in a local food store, one of the students persuaded the maid to let him into Ted's room. There he did two things: knowing of Ted's practice of taking a warm bath and jumping directly in the bed without PJ's, the student sprinkled the unflavored gelatin crystals on his bed sheet; then he poured about half of the coffee creamer out and replaced it with the gelatin crystals. The two phased payback was in place.

Several students waited in the hallway until Ted completed his bath and rushed to jump into bed because of the winter cold. A loud, "What the (expletive deleted) is in my bed?" We all waited for breakfast. Ted as usual refused to share the creamer. He put three heaping teaspoons of his creamer in his small cup of coffee and stirred. Continuing with his meal, Ted reached for the coffee cup to see the spoon standing straight up in a thick, dark paste. The English waiter was also confounded, but later had a big laugh when someone explained about the gelatin and the reason for the joke.

159 "C-A-RRRA- BO-LICA   AC- SID"

Speaking at a Mexican camp for college students one summer on the Gulf of California, I gained some insight into the Hispanic culture. When I arrived at the beach camp there were three tent structures. The central one was for meetings and eating. Some of the staff also slept there. On each side of the central tent was a tent for the college girls and the college boys with staff in the middle.

It was a task in the heat to teach and interface the group especially working through an interpreter. My material had been translated into Spanish, but I did not feel comfortable attempting to teach in other than English. Most of the college students knew English anyway. During the third day of the camp, a group of young Mexicans on motorcycles arrived because they heard that there were college girls on the beach. Most of the staff were frightened by this gang-type appearance and were unwilling to confront the men. I was asked to speak to the motorcycle group and explain that it was a religious camp and that the meeting was limited to the group present (no visitors were allowed).

I approached the obvious group leader and asked in broken Spanish if he could speak English. He could not, so I told him in Spanish that English was not difficult because little children spoke English. He laughed and shared that little children speak Spanish in Mexico, too! Asked if he wanted to learn English, the leader answered, "Si!"

"Repeat after me, 'c- a- rrra- bo-lica ac-sid.'" He repeated, "c- a- rrra- bo-lica ac-sid." "Bueno," I said . . ."andar rapidimento!" I attempted to communicate that the words "carbolic acid" meant to "go rapidly." He got the message. I asked him to teach it to the others. He began, "c- a- rrra- bo-lica ac-sid." They all began to laugh and started their motorcycles and rode away. Was I lucky, or did God just work a miracle? I was a hero for about fifteen minutes, in my own mind.

160 I SAW A SHOE TONGUE IN THE STEW

Following my meeting with the motorcycle gang, it was lunch time. Mexican stew had been prepared in a #10 wash tub. I think I saw a tennis shoe tongue in the stew. Not having a missionary stomach, I ask for some alternative.

A young missionary intern and I was prepared a fish dinner, Mexican style. The fish was cooked just as it was taken from the water and placed on a plate with the eye looking straight at the eater. I took a tortilla, tore it in half, put one half over the fish eye and the other half over the tail. Then I proceeded to eat carefully in between. The intern followed my example.

Both of us got some strange looks, but it was better than tennis shoe tongue stew. (Later I was told it was a beef tongue, but that didn't make a difference). Years later the young intern became a missionary leader in Central and South America. The last time I saw him I asked if he ever became able to eat Mexican fish without the tortilla. He smiled and said, "It took awhile, but I finally developed a missionary stomach. Early on, following your example, I offended some before someone explained to me how to eat fish cooked Mexican style."

161   PRAYING FOR PEDRO

Traveling from Europe all the way to Rio de Janeiro to speak at a World Missions Conference was exciting. I looked forward to the service, but was a bit disappointed when I realized it was a small local church with about seventy people in attendance. The crowd was small, but the lessons I learned from this small church about missions, evangelism, and caring and praying for one another have been part of my ministry ever since. In fact, I developed a "Pray for Pedro" program for intercessory prayer from a central lesson of the meeting. The opportunity to travel so far to speak was exciting, but God had a larger reason for the invitation. The small crowd and the lessons learned humbled me.

It seems the little church had a custom to draw names at the annual missions meeting for a "secret pal" person for whom to pray until the next annual meeting. Each person present put their name in a basket at the beginning of the service. At the time of the offering, individuals would come forward to put their mission gifts in a basket and announce the person for whom they had prayed during the past year. Some would provide insights as to how God led them to pray. Others would explain how blessed they had been during their times of prayer for the person whose name they had drawn.

The service was in Portuguese. The pastor interpreted for me. One lady came forward and after giving her missions offering, said, "Last March 14, in the early morning hours, I was awakened with a burden to pray for [she told the name of the person she had drawn]." She said she prayed for over an hour until the burden lifted. At that moment, the man she had named stood and said, "That was the night the brakes failed on my truck, and I nearly ran off the mountain!" It was easy to see how God had used prayer to bring the small congregation together.

After most everyone had come forward, an elderly man named Pedro came forward. He was crippled in one leg and one arm. He was a street sweeper in the city. He said, "This year I pray for Pedro!" [If one were to draw their own name, they were instructed to replace it and draw again, but South America was full of people named, Pedro.] Pedro said, "This year I pray for Pedro. I don't know which Pedro I prayed for, maybe I prayed for myself."

At that moment I saw the real value of intercessory prayer: one cannot pray for others without receiving benefits themselves. Since this exposure to intercessory prayer, I have included a program "PRAYING FOR PEDRO" in churches across America. The testimonies of answered prayers, personal spiritual growth from praying for others, and the fruits of spiritual renewal at the congregational level have been a source of real encouragement to me through the years. Here is a sample:

"Pray for Pedro" Project
New Life Baptist Church, Bluff City, Tennessee

This project is designed to provide each person who is willing to pray for others a special person to intercede for them during the next thirty days. It operates on the Golden Rule for prayer: "Pray for others as you want them to pray for you."

IF YOU ARE WILLING TO SELECT A NAME AND PRAY FOR THE NEXT 30 DAYS, print your name below:

PEDRO:_____

"As I pray for my PEDRO, it is good to know someone is praying for me. Thank you for your prayers and concern. God bless you as you pray for me!"

Normally, the pastor arranges for each PEDRO to report to the church the person for whom they have been praying. This is usually scheduled in about thirty days after the first drawing. The next time a church draws names, it is for ninety days. Then when the program is well established, they draw names for one year. Prayer enhances one's spiritual memories. Prayer works wonders in the hearts of those who pray. Pray for Pedro! It works!

I shared the PRAY FOR PEDRO program in a church in St. Croix, USVI and spoke about intercessory payer and that one could not pray for others without receiving a blessing themselves. At the close of a Sunday through Wednesday meeting a young girl, about 10 or 11, wrote me a letter:

"Dear Dr. Green, I like your preaching. I like stories about people's lives. I enjoyed Mrs. Green's singing; it was warm and soft and comfortable. And prayer is just like jam. You can't spread even a little without getting some on yourself." [Children do understand the message!]

See #189 "WHO THE HELL IS PEDRO?"

162   MONEY CHANGERS IN LIMA

Traveling in South America, I stopped for a few days in Lima, Peru. There was a monetary crisis in the country, and currency exchange could legally be transacted only in a bank. Yet, there were Peruvians who went to great lengths attempting to acquire dollars. The first night I awoke with a man in my room. Startled, I asked, "What are you doing here?" [I discovered the door lock didn't work.]

He wanted to give me a real deal on money exchange. I dismissed him outright. The next evening a woman showed up in my room with another story attempting to get dollars. The following night, I placed a chair under the door knob and balanced the metal waste can on the chair. About the same time that evening, the trash can fell to the floor. It woke me, but also startled the person attempting to gain entrance to my room. I decided to continue my journey and leave Peru as quickly as possible. Travel could be great fun if you didn't have to deal with such people.

163   CUSTOMS AND THE BOOKS

On an annual trip to Oxford, England, I found a large book sale. Searching for titles of value to the school library, I purchased more than I could adequately carry aboard the plane home. Mother was along and only had one suitcase even though she was allowed two. I bought another suitcase and checked it on the plane as Mother's luggage. Passing through customs, Mother was randomly selected for luggage inspection. Mother was eighty-five years old, so the Customs Inspector assisted her by lifting her two suitcases off the luggage cart to the inspection table. The customs man asked, "What in the world do you have in here?" Mother answered, "Books, I read a lot!" He opened the bag and took a look at a couple of the books and said, "That's some heavy reading!" Mother did read a lot, so she considered her answer truthful.

164 STAIN GLASS WINDOWS IN A SUIT BAG

I was in England looking for church furniture items for a planned chapel at Oxford Graduate School in Tennessee. I found two small stained glass windows at an Oxford flea market. They were colorful depictions of the rising sun that had been removed from an old building in the city. The gentleman from whom they were purchased taped them together and wrapped them in newspaper. When I started home, I put them in my carry on suit bag with my suits hanging on both sides as protection. At the exit customs, the Inspector noticed the bag looked heavy and asked what I had in it. "Stain glass windows for my school chapel," I answered. "Sorry, I asked," was his response. He waived me through with a smile.

Those two stain glass windows were installed above the raised pulpit in the chapel in honor of some English friends. The windows, together with an English Pulpit, a 17th Century Baptismal Font, and other items from St. Michael's at the North Gate, the City Church of Oxford [the oldest church in the city] grace the English chapel on campus. When I see the windows and other historical items in the Chapel, I often think of their long journey from Old England to the campus of Oxford Graduate School in Tennessee. If they could speak, what stories they could tell.

165 GEORGE AND THE PRISSY WAITRESS

George D. Finigan, EdD, DPhil, was a colleague and friend. One day in London, UK, we were waiting to be seated in a

restaurant. The waitress motioned to us, "Walk this way."
George observed her prissy walk and whispered to me, "If I
could walk that way, I wouldn't need talcum powder." George
was a former Marine and was converted to Christianity late in
his academic career. I thought nothing of George's remarks.
It was just George, being George!

166   I RECEIVED A HONG KONG PACKAGE

Traveling in the Asia/Pacific area, I arrived three days
early in Hong Kong for a most welcome rest. Walking through
the airport, I heard, "Brother Green is that you?" It was
a missionary from the Philippines. His second question was,
"Where are you staying? I'll change hotels so we can visit."
I was fearful that my rest was gone. He came to my room
and talked until after midnight. I guess it is always good to
talk with people from back home.

The next day I decided to go shopping, but it was a
Chinese Holiday, and the shops were closed. I had promised
to buy a British Racing Cap and a sleeveless cashmere
sweater vest for a friend. Even though the shops were
closed, I decided to do some window shopping just to pass
the time alone. Looking in the window of a shop that carried
the items I wanted to purchase, I was feeling somewhat
discouraged since I would leave Hong Kong before the shops
opened.

Standing outside the shop was a well dressed gentleman
who asked, "Do you wish to purchase something?" "Yes, but
the shops are closed." He was the owner of the shop and
said he would take my order and mail it to me. I told him
the items I wanted and the sizes. He asked for my mailing
address and said it will be $37.18. Without thinking I paid
the man and took a copy of the order and returned to the

hotel wondering how stupid can one be giving money on the street to a stranger.

At the hotel I spoke to the concierge and told him what I had done. He asked for my mailing address and the amount I paid the merchant. Then he wrote me a personal guarantee. "If you do not receive the merchandise within 21 days, I will personally send you the $37.18. Hong Kong merchants are the most honest people in the world. This is how they build their business."

In less than 3 weeks a package came from Hong Kong with the merchandise and a small envelope. The envelope contained a note and 17 cents. It seems the merchant had overestimated the postage. I could hardly believe it. Never before or since have I witnessed such business integrity. I trust this remains true.

Section Four
Preachers and the Ministry

167 A MEETING OF MALE TITHE PAYERS

When I was about twelve, the pastor called a special meeting for "male tithe payers." In my church, this was a serious meeting. Since Mother had taught me to tithe on the odd jobs I did in the community, I decided to attend the meeting. When the pastor arrived and saw me on the front seat, he asked one of the deacons to explain to me that the meeting was about some trouble in the church and that the meeting was for adults only.

The Brother came to me with the pastor's message, and I responded, "The meeting was for tithe paying male members. So I came." He explained further that the meeting was to discuss some moral problems with some church leadership and that the adults felt uncomfortable discussing the matter with me present. Ira Johnson overheard the deacon talking with me and stood up and told the group, "If he is old enough to join the church, he is old enough to learn both the good and the bad. How do you expect young men to learn both sides of the issue if they can't attend important meetings? How can they ever learn to be leaders in the church if they can't see both sides?"

The deacon and the pastor had a discussion and decided that I could stay. The nature of the discussion about the personal behavior of two members and how it affected the church was a good lesson for me to learn. It became obvious that even Christians have human problems and need understanding and forgiveness. This lesson provided an early perspective on the Christian life and the church that I needed then and now.

168 I BAPTIZED A FEW CHICKENS

My decision to become a minister was made before I became a teenager. Being so young and having to wait so long to begin preparation for the ministry made me impatient. I decided to practice a little on my own. My paternal Grandfather, Alexander Little Page Green, (1874-1963), had a large stock pond near his barn, so I decided to practice baptizing.

Finding no suitable candidates, all that was left were chickens or cats. I caught two cats and three chickens and decided that was enough to have a Baptismal Service. I turned the cats loose because I couldn't think of anything religious to say about cats. Chickens were a different story. I had heard lots of stories about preachers eating so much chicken. This gave me the idea that some chickens entered the ministry almost every Sunday.

I still remember one of Grandfather's chicken stories about the preacher who came home with a farmer for Sunday dinner. After eating, the pastor and the farmer were sitting on the porch, and a large rooster began to crow. The preacher asked, "What's got into that rooster crowing this time of day?" The farmer replied, "He is proud. He had two sons enter the ministry today."

With each baptism, I made a speech about the individual chicken trusting Christ and mentioned the possibility that the chicken may enter the ministry at some future date. This I did with some loud praying. Then I baptized each one in the Name of the Father, and of the Son, and of the Holy Ghost. This I had learned from church.

One of my cousins, who will remain nameless, [we now call him Johnnie NoCash] told Grandfather what I was doing. He came and watched a while, then suggested that I should wait until I was older with more education or till I was ordained and had some more appropriate candidates. I thought I was in trouble, but Grandfather actually encouraged me in my preparation for ministry. He did think I was a little young to actually begin making Baptists out of all the barnyard animals. He was a Methodist. That's when I first learned that there was competition between denominations.

Looking back, baptizing a few chickens was a good start. I now could report three baptisms, if anyone asked. In fact, many children do not understand the true meaning of the sacraments observed in the church. To illustrate: following church one rainy Sunday after a little girl had witnessed her first water baptism, she was dunking her rag doll in a mud hole in the yard. When her mother observed more closely, the little girl was saying, "In the name of the Father, and the Son, and in the hole you go."

No one took time to explain the order or importance of baptism as identification with the Trinity. Adults should take care to see that the meanings of religious practices are clear and that the children understand.

169   MY FIRST CAR

My first car was a 1939 Plymouth business coupe that had belonged to an old maid school teacher. It had never been driven over 35 miles an hour and looked new. I remember the payment well; it was $32 a month and was hard to make. Sometimes Mother would help me. On my first short trip, I had a problem. For a young man in his first car with almost no money, it was a big problem. When I drove with a little speed, oil somehow got into the radiator. What could cause such a problem?

A mechanic explained that the oil was not draining back into the oil case. When I told him it had belonged to an old teacher, he understood the problem. The years of slow driving had allowed the rings to clog up. When he told me it had to have a ring job, I was crushed. Sharing my financial bind with the mechanic, he said if what I told him were true about the car, that when I got home to take the car to someone I trusted and ask the mechanic to just take the head off, replace the rings, and put it back together. This would keep the cost down, but it might not work. Was I willing to take the risk? I was pleased when it worked that no one tried to take advantage of a young man.

There comes a time in life when someone has to be trusted. I trusted the elderly woman who sold me the car. I trusted the mechanic who said it could be fixed. The car was fixed, and it worked fine. I was ready for the world! Those were the days when people could be trusted. An individual's word was their bond. Why can't it be that way today?

170 THAT'S MY DOG, "MOREOVER"

Early in my ministry, I spoke at a youth service in Alabama. Knowing my interest in dogs, Max Morris, a young pianist in the church, offered to take me to see a special dog. This dog belonged to an old preacher who gave the dog a biblical name. When we arrived, the preacher immediately said, "You came to see my dogs, didn't you?" He took us to his main dog and said, "I call this dog, 'Moreover.' His name comes from the Bible. You know, over there where 'Moreover' the dogs came and licked the sores of Lazarus." A Bible name for a dog, now that's a stretch, but I understood it was the old preacher's means to share a message. The old man no longer had a pulpit, but he still had a message to share with anyone who would listen. If God can use a donkey or cause the rocks to praise Him, why not

an old preacher using a dog to point people to a passage of
scripture. Whatever it takes!

171   THE TENT PREACHER

When I was attending Beckley College in West Virginia,
a tent preacher came to town. Attending with some of
the students, we were surprised that an uneducated man
could confuse scripture and still teach valuable lessons. He
obviously could not read, so his wife read the Scripture on
which he gave commentary in his so called sermon.

The first night the wife read from Galatians 6:1, "Oh,
thou foolish Galatians, who hath 'be-switched you." The
actual word was "bewitched," but he took his cue from her
pronunciation and preached, "Don't let the devil switch you on
a sidetrack." He spoke of the main railway line and the spur
tracks that led to the coal mines. He told the people to stay
on the mainline and that the sidetrack just goes to a hole in
the ground. It was an awful good sermon; it communicated a
valuable lesson!

The next night the wife read someplace about people who
"creep in unaware" so he picked up on her reading and said,
"Some will creep in under the wire without repenting of their
sins." He preached about people joining the church without
being saved. Also, about people seeking water baptism without
repentance and said, "I don't care if you are baptized until
every fish in the river knows you by name, that won't save
you without repentance!"

The other nights I attended were equally revealing. He
shared that it was better to be the "Head and not the Tail"
and spoke of keeping up and not lagging behind. March at
the head of the parade, don't bring up the rear! "Don't let
the Lord lay you off" was another sermon. He declared,
"Essential workers are never laid off." He challenged the

people to be effective workers and be active in witnessing. He didn't say it exactly in those words, but the words he used definitely spoke to the people present.

The old preacher told us that God even used a donkey, he said "a Jack Ass!" when the prophet would not carry the message. He also reminded the people that even the rocks and the trees would cry out if the truth were not declared. God can use anyone willing to repeat His message. I came to understand that education and oratory were not necessary to share spiritual truth. An honest heart with good intentions was sufficient to witness. In addition to a divine call, education assisted in the preparation of material, but the oratory must be inspired by God to be effective. I trust God will give the church more plain spoken individuals who will not flinch from declaring what they believe to be the whole counsel of God.

172   A VISIT BY A DEVIL OR SOMETHING

My first year of youth ministry (1951) was hectic. Dealing with various congregations, staying in different homes, eating different food, adjusting to weather, and spiritual battles, it was a lonesome trail. The greatest of these battles was in the midst of a fall youth revival in Coal City, West Virginia. I was staying with the J. H. Hughes family and sleeping in an upstairs bedroom. They had a son, Dale, about my age who was still in school. We became friends and played practical jokes on each other.

One morning after going to the bathroom I returned to get a few more winks. With my eyes closed, lying on my back, I felt the presence of someone in the room. Assuming it to be Dale, I decided to play opossum and see what he would do. I was certain it was some kind of practical joke. My arm was lifted, my pulse taken, and I began choking. Realizing that someone had a hand on my throat, I took it as long as I could and then opened my eyes, tried to yell, and sat up in bed. There was no one there! It was scary. I reached for my Bible on the nightstand and clutched it to my chest and began praying as if I were sinking on the Titanic.

An extremely loud noise was heard just outside the upper bedroom window. At this sound, the father, a large man, rushed into my room. Seeing me white and trembling with fright, he said, "I heard the noise and thought the big tree had fallen on the house." His first thought was that Dale and I were playing more of our games, but Dale was still asleep. He examined my arm and neck and declared, "The Devil has been here!" I really don't know what happened. The spirit world is real, and if God can intervene in the lives of men...so can the forces of Evil. It pays to be prepared. Having a Bible and a friend handy is good insurance, too.

173   A TAXI TO THE WRONG CHURCH

My first attempt at speaking for a youth meeting outside of Tennessee was in Bald Knob, Arkansas. I traveled by train all night from Chattanooga, stopping at every local station before arriving at Bald Knob about 9 AM on Sunday. Tired but not wanting to be late I took a taxi to the church. When I arrived it was a church much larger than I expected. When I met the pastor he was very kind but said "Son, the taxi brought you to the wrong church, but I will drive you over to the other side of town to the church where you are supposed to be." When I arrived the church was small with only 67 people present (I was disappointed), but pleased to have an opportunity to speak. That was the beginning of a long traveling and speaking journey that took me to 103 countries and into many different denominations. I have always considered myself to be a New Testament Christian not tied to a particular sectarian position. This opened many doors for me to share my personal ministry.

174   YOU USE TOO MUCH BIBLE

My ministry began as a teenager. Traveling and speaking to youth groups was exciting. At every opportunity I discussed my speaking with anyone of experience. I learned many things along the way to two doctorates: one in theology and another in philosophy, but the hardest lesson to learn about my personal preaching came from a pastor in Seaford, Delaware. At the conclusion of a youth revival, I stayed a few days to discuss my ministry. It was an effort to improve my preparation. His main criticism was that I had a good memory and quoted too many Bible verses in my sermons. I was devastated. How could one use too much scripture? He explained that as I matured and learned more about life I would have things to say myself and would not have to depend totally on verses I could find in the Bible.

From that moment forward, I took every opportunity that came my way to get a better education. First, a bachelor's degree in Biblical Studies, then a seminary degree in Divinity, a masters in Religious Education, a doctorate in Theology, and finally a university doctorate in Philosophy with a major in Education and Social Change. I wanted something to say, but my education never replaced the Bible in my speaking. In fact a Texas church member complimented me by saying, "He preaches like he doesn't even have an education." Certainly, I became a different kind of preacher using fewer verses and spending more quality time expressing the Bible in my own words and making application. At times I did have more to say, but I was never convinced that what I had to say was equal to what God said in the scripture. I took to heart the constructive criticism, but tried to keep the Bible central to my thinking and sermon development.

175   TIED TO MOTHER'S APRON STRINGS

With Father's death in 1937, Mother was left to raise and educate three children; times were hard for the family. When I decided to become a minister, my maternal Grandfather, Robert Tate Curton, (1877-1955), was upset. He thought that I should get a job and support my widowed mother. He wanted Mother to tie me to her apron strings and ask me to get a regular job and stay home.

Mother would have nothing to do with that approach. Although Mother did not want me to be a minister, she was convinced that I believed God had called me, and she was careful about interfering with God's plans. Mother's main concern was really the expression of her father's attitude. Pastors are not appreciated, they do not make much money, and their positions are usually insecure. She wanted something more than that for her only son. Yet, as God used her son, she became a strong supporter of the work and ministry to which God guided me.

176   GRANDMOTHER'S POSTCARD

My paternal Grandmother Mattie Barton Green, (1883-1966), was the strongest source of encouragement for my early ministry. She liked the idea of me being a preacher and constantly shared her feelings with me about the whole process. After I started traveling in youth work, she would arrange to have "a little money" each time I dropped by her house. She would hand it to me and say, "This is not my tithe; I put tithes in my local church. This is an offering to help you get to your next church meeting." Those few dollars were a big help, but her attitude was worth even more.

When I couldn't come by for awhile, she would write me a penny postcard. It was great the way she wrote small letters and filled the whole back with words then continued on the front of the post card. She would go around the edge line after line until there was only a small space left for the address. How I wish I had kept some of those postcards. They were such a blessing! Many years have passed, and as I remember her kindness and encouragement, I gain strength to continue the journey.

177   HE'LL SAY THINGS NOT IN THE BIBLE

My mother did not hear me preach until about twelve years after my first sermon. She would say, "He's too young. He'll say things that are not even in the Bible." My mother became Dean of Women at a college, and I was invited to speak for Religious Emphasis Week. Mother was still afraid that I had not learned enough to preach a proper sermon. Believing God was guiding me, I chose carefully the material for the series.

The first day, as I read the scripture passage that was to frame my remarks, I did a free translation to make it more meaningful to a college audience. About a few select words, I mentioned the deeper meaning from the Greek text and spoke of the original intent of the writer. Mother turned to a colleague and said, "See he is saying things that are not even in my Bible."

The series went well, and I was complimented by the faculty. Everyone seemed to enjoy my preaching but Mother. Many years passed, and Mother finally told me how proud she was that I had become such a fine preacher. She said, "You used to be Grace's son, now I am Dr. Green's mother." It was her way of saying, "You're doing a good job. Keep up the good work."

178 FROM WHAT BOOK?

Speaking at a national youth convention in Virginia some years ago, my former pastor came up to me and asked, "From what book did you get that sermon?" My answer was simply, "The Bible!" He insisted on knowing what book, so I said, "Matthew." He asked what book of sermons I had read to get the ideas. I pulled out my Greek New Testament and read Matthew 28:10 to him in Greek. "That's where I got the ideas!" It seems that parents and preachers never realize that young people grow up, become educated, get new ideas, and start thinking for themselves.

The sermon in question was on the Great Commission. It is amazing how a misunderstanding became self-defeating and produced a theology of coercion. This was an effort to compel people to "go and do" when they should be "making disciples as they went about their daily life." I had explained that the "go" of the commission was really a participle and not an imperative and should be translated "going" or "as you go." Christ knew His followers would go, so He gave them a program: as you personally go into all the world "make disciples." The commission was for believers already in motion. The "go ye" was in their hearts not the results of a minister's urging.

They did not need preachers to challenge and push them toward involvement. They needed only to be encouraged to practice a Christian lifestyle. The pastor's questions suggested that old preachers never believe that young men can become scholars and teach them a new perspective. As young preachers begin to think for themselves, the church has a chance at renewal.

179   I LIKE GOOD PREACHING

Early in my ministry I had a pastorate in South Carolina. A young man with some obvious limitations often sat on the front seat during the Sunday morning service. He had a unique memory for a short period. After the service, this young man would often go to the front steps of the church and repeat, word for word, my sermon. These were the days before recorders were in common use, so I would rush out the side door and around to the front of the Church. Most people thought I was coming around to shake hands with the congregation as they exited the building. The truth was I rushed to hear the young man repeat my sermon. It was most inspirational. I always loved good preaching!

180   JUST BEEN EXHORTING

Many years ago, I was appointed to serve on a committee to examine an individual for a "local preaching license." He was required to complete an extensive form for review by the committee. I was amazed at the "honesty" of this man. He was a late bloomer religiously, and it was doubtful that he would make it in the ministry. His education was limited and his natural gifts were few, but he had a large dose of candor. Sometimes he was confused by the questions, but mostly he was frank and open with his answers.

On the question of sex, where he should have written "male" he wrote "2 or 3 times a week." To the question, "How long have you been preaching?" he answered, "Ain't been preaching, just exhorting." His most forthright and honest answer was to the question, "Have you been faithful to your wife since your marriage?" The simple answer was, "No." I had never witnessed such honesty.

Since honesty is the best policy, the committee gave him an opportunity to do a "little exhorting" in the inner-city mission. He put his whole heart and soul into each message at the mission. The men responded to his enthusiasm and his unorthodox style. It is wonderful how God chooses and uses different folks with different strokes. He was a living example to the inner-city mission of what God could do when one totally surrenders to divine guidance. Hopefully, God will provide a few more honest men for the ministry who experienced a life changing relationship with Christ.

181   THE JAWBONE OF A DONKEY

As a young minister I was scheduled to speak to a national youth convention. Most of the delegates were teenagers, and I prepared carefully for the message. My effort was to challenge them to use what they had at hand to "fight the good fight of faith." I shared how young David had used five stones to win the battle against Goliath, the giant; how Shamgar used an ox goad to kill 600 Philistines and saved Israel; and how Samson used the jawbone of an ass to kill 1,000 of the enemy.

At this point, I wanted to be careful not to use the word "ass," so I substituted "donkey," and this is how it came out: "Samson took the jawbone of a donkey and beat the ass off a thousand Philistines!" You guessed it; the teenagers rolled in the aisles. This was in the Sixties when the vocabulary of Christian young people was extremely limited. These teens had never heard someone from the pulpit talk about "beating the ass off somebody." They exploded in laughter. In my youthful ignorance, I didn't know what happened. I turned to the folk in charge with a puzzled look. One member of the convening clergy said, "Just close the service." This we did, but the laughter continued.

Many years later, Gail and I were having lunch with a Florida couple when he told the story of someone speaking at a youth convention and getting his tongue on his eye teeth and saying, "Samson took the jawbone of a donkey and beat the ass off a thousand Philistines." Gail sheepishly asked, "Did you know that was Hollis?" We had a good laugh.

Of all the stories told about my ministry, Gail's Grandmother Parks enjoyed the jawbone story most. She lived to be ninety-two years old and many times asked me to tell her "the jawbone story." It was the kind of slip of the tongue that both young and old enjoyed. After the initial embarrassment, I have enjoyed telling the story myself. In fact, on her death-bed Grandmother Parks asked me to tell her again about the "jawbone."

182   MY GOD! WHAT A COW!

I had a great uncle, Bill Curton, who was a Methodist circuit riding preacher. One particular church on his rural charge was in a rough and tough mountain community. The young men were always pulling pranks on the traveling preacher. On one occasion they hooked a team of mules to the corner pillar of the church, and during the sermon, pulled the post out and caused the small frame church to lean sideways. On Uncle Bill's next circuit visit to that church, he brought a 12-gage shotgun and a pistol. He placed the shotgun against the pulpit and laid the pistol next to his Bible and said, "I came here to preach!"

As a circuit rider, Preacher Bill wanted a glass of nourishing milk instead of water on the pulpit. The next Sunday those same boys spiked the milk with local white-lightning "moonshine." The story goes that as Bill preached he took a sip of the spiked milk and remarked, "My God! What a cow!" Before the long sermon ended, Bill suggested that he buy this special cow, tie it to his horse, and take it along with him so he could enjoy this special mountain milk.

The rest of the story: sharing this story in a publication. A Japanese man, Isao Ebihara, sent an email asking, "What kind of lightning did they put in that preacher's milk?" I guess everyone in the world don't know about mountain moonshine or the atmospheric electrostatic discharge accompanied by the ingestion of such home-made shine.

183   THE PREACHER'S BLIND MULE

My paternal Grandfather A.L.P. Green told me about a rural Methodist pastor plowing his garden with a blind mule. Each time he gave a command to the blind mule he would use several names: get up, John, Jack, Bob, and Bill. One day a member of his congregation came by and asked why he used so many names when all he had was one blind mule. The old pastor said, "Shh, he thinks he has somebody helping him." The member didn't understand, so the preacher explained, "You see, the church selects leaders to assist the pastor with the church, but it usually falls back on the preacher. I call all those names to encourage the old mule that someone is helping him pull the plow." I guess this idea works for appointed committees; several names are called so the Chair thinks someone is assisting with committee work. Anyway, that's one of my grandfather's stories. He was a great story teller.

184   THROW THAT DOG OUT

During the morning sermon one Sunday, a pastor of a church in Chattanooga, Tennessee, noticed a dog in the aisle. He called for the deacons to "Throw that dog out of the House of God!" After the service a lady told the preacher,

"You shouldn't have put that blind man's seeing eye dog out of the church." The preacher went straight to the visitor and apologized. The visitor's response, "Oh, that's O.K. preacher, that sermon wasn't fit for my dog to hear any way!" I guess that expressed the visitor's evaluation of both the meeting and the message.

185   THE HUGGING LADIES

After ministering in a Jacksonville Church, I stood with the pastor, H. G. Poitier, at the rear of the black church while several beautiful young ladies in the line began to hug the old pastor. He was a handsome old gentleman, Sidney Poitier's uncle, and had been their pastor for many years. They had grown up under his ministry, so they gave him a full bosom grandfather hug. As they came to me, I took a step back and extended my hand.

Some reluctantly shook my hand, but one beautiful young black lady insisted on hugging me. I said, "I'm not sure my ordination can handle such a hug!" Her response was clear: "You white folks make sin out of everything!" I agreed that ministers sometimes erred on the side of caution. She mumbled something that sounded like, "You folks can't tell the difference between Christian love and other stuff." All the old preachers that spoke to me about my ministry always cautioned me about over familiarity with females. My thoughts were "...it's better to be safe than sorry."

186   THE PRAYER ANSWERING DOG

Just as I was introduced to speak at a convention in Jacksonville, Florida, an usher lady all dressed in white sashayed down the aisle. She was speaking aloud, "Don't murder anybody; God said don't kill anybody." Being the only white person present, I kept the pulpit between me and the lady. As she continued to shout her refrain, she put her hand into a brown paper bag. I took another step back.

Then she continued, "My daughter wanted to come to this meeting, but she didn't have any shoes. So we prayed..." Then she pulled out a sandal with dog teeth marks on it and showed it to the congregation. "My dog, Rusty, done found this shoe. My daughter couldn't come to this meeting with one shoe, so we prayed again." Pulling the mate to the sandal out of the paper bag, she began to rejoice about Rusty finding two shoes that matched.

After a few moments of rejoicing by the congregation about this prayer answering dog, one large deacon stood up in the choir and said, "If Rusty ever has any pups, I want one!" Another Brother responded, "It might not be in the blood line; Sister, could I borrow Rusty for a few days? I sure do need some prayers answered!" In all it was a memorable introduction to a message about a God big enough to meet our needs!

187   THE SHOUTING FARMER

My maternal Grandfather, Robert Tate Curton, told me about an old gentleman in Yellow Creek Baptist Church who constantly shouted, "Amen! Praise the Lord! Glory! Hallelujah!" at almost everything that was said from the pulpit. This plagued the church for several months until the deacons, in an attempt to quiet the old man, told him if he wouldn't shout for a month they would buy him a new pair of boots.

A few days later, as the old man plowed his garden, a deacon stopped by to check on him. The deacon began to explain how good God had been to the old man in blessing his crop. After several minutes of the deacon talking about

God's blessings, the old man said loudly, "Hold my mule!
Boots or no boots --I've got to shout!" I guess a good
feeling deep down in the soul is better than a new pair of
boots and makes real the verse "From the abundance of the
heart the mouth speaks!" I guess a righteous soul will find a
way to express the deep joy that is in the heart.

188 PREACHER PULL YOURSELF TOGETHER

I grew up in an exciting church in Chattanooga, Tennessee.
There was lots of singing and rejoicing about the goodness
of God. One Sunday morning, a visiting preacher got
excited and said, "I'm so happy! I know my feet are on
the floor, but I feel like my head is in the heavens!" A
Brother whispered, "Preacher, pull yourself together." A
few snickers could be heard, but one thing was sure: that
preacher was a happy camper. I always enjoyed a preacher
with a little humor.

189 "WHO THE HELL IS PEDRO?"

Hazel Porter and daughters, Deanna and Leanne, were
among those at Grandview Baptist Church who took the
Pray for Pedro program seriously (see #161). I reminded
the children who wanted to draw names, that they must be
conscientious and pray every day for their "secret prayer
pal." Leanne, about 10 years old at the time, prayed for
her Pedro several times each day, even putting a sticker on
the bathroom mirror. At meals she would always add to the
grace, "and God bless Pedro." At bedtime she would remind
the family, "Don't forget to pray for Pedro." Observing his
young daughter continually praying for some stranger, her
father could no longer hold back the question, "Who the hell
is Pedro, and what's wrong with him?!"

Over the years, many prayers had been made on behalf of "Blackie" Porter, but the fervent prayers of a child helped to soften his heart. Observation, a question asked in exasperation, a family communicating, and the way was prepared. One Wednesday evening when none of the family attended prayer meeting, Gail and I dropped by the Porter home to find Blackie sitting in the yard. He explained that he was going to the hospital for lung biopsy the next morning.

"Blackie, are you ready to go?," I asked. "No," he answered simply. "Weren't you a member of Wolf Creek Church and baptized when you were a teenager?" "Yes," he said, "But it didn't take." We prayed together to make his "calling and election sure." By Friday, Blackie was dead. Praying for Pedro had raised his awareness that it is never too late to make things right with God.

190   CHAIN OF COMMAND

During a Christmas program at Grandview Baptist Church, four little brothers sat on the front pew. As the youngest became restless, Gail almost lost it when she overheard an older brother whisper: "Be still! The preacher will see you, and he will tell God then God will tell Santa Claus." If we better understood a child's chain of command, we could communicate with them more effectively about the core values they need to learn. One tragedy of American family life is the loss of the real meaning of religious holidays. Children are not being taught these things at home or at church.

191 THE REAL MEANING OF CHRISTMAS

Samuel Kibera came to America to further his education. On one trip home to Kenya, he returned with his family. They came to the Christmas program at Grandview Baptist Church directly from the airport. The four small African boys, who had never been in a church surrounded by white faces, were placed down front so they could see the program. A Sunday school teacher, knowing they were coming, placed presents under the tree for each of the children.

At the end of the program, the first present had the name of the youngest Kibera child. When he heard his name, disbelief covered his face. As the teacher handed him a large plastic truck, he contemplated the gift. Having been taught that good things come from Jesus, he stood up on the pew, turned to the audience, raised the truck in the air, and said in a loud voice, "Jesus! Jesus!" He had learned the true meaning of Christmas. Hopefully, other children got the message, maybe some parents, too.

192 WORLD IS GOING TO HELL IN A BOAT

Driving one summer, Glendon Hale and I were listening to a series of preachers on their Saturday morning radio broadcasts. They came on one after the other with the following one trying to out-preach or correct the false teachings of the previous one. Finally, we could take no more and were about to turn to another station when a preacher arrived late for his short broadcast because of traffic going to the lake.

The radio preacher rushed to the microphone out of breath. After a moment of silence he said, "I believe the whole world is going to hell in a boat!" Had it not been serious, it would have been hilarious. He declared, I doubt there will be any boats on the "lake of fire" in Hell. Anyway it explained why he was late arriving to the station.

193   A PORTION OF MY TIES

A radio preacher on WOAY, in Oak Hill, West Virginia, had the custom of asking listeners to send a portion of their tithes to assist his ministry. He usually opened his mail on the air, especially those that appeared to have money, so he could announce the name of the donor. I was listening one Saturday morning as he opened mail and came across a "fat" letter.

With great expectation he opened the envelope "on the air" to find a note which said, "Here is a portion of my ties!" Several pieces of old neck ties cut about the size of dollar bills were wrapped and included in the envelope. I suppose the word "tithes" and "ties" sound alike on the radio. Surely the preacher was disappointed. I doubt those "ties" would match any of his suits. In fact, he didn't even wear ties. He was an "open-collar" preacher.

194   AN ENCORE FOR DISCORD

My friend, Glendon Hale, and I decided to visit a broadcast of a radio preacher to see what it was all about. After arriving, we were asked to sing. Since my friend played the piano and I sang a little, we agreed. Finally we settled on a song, but Glendon couldn't play it in my key. He said he would try to transpose. The people insisted that we perform anyway.

My friend attempted to transpose, but it didn't work. He played the song in his favorite key, and I sang it in another key. It was a discordant mess, but the audience wanted an encore. We decided against another effort so the preacher would have more time to preach. That was a big mistake! Obviously, the people wanted another song to take up time because the preacher had almost nothing to say...at least, not much worth listening to anyway.

We should have responded to the applause and done the same song again. The audience would have loved us! The preacher got mail requesting us to sing on future programs, but we were afraid it would lead to a celebrated career in gospel music or something. After all, we didn't want to become stars in the music business. It is a hard life, with lots of traveling, hardly ever sleeping in your own bed...and sometimes your head grows bigger than it should. Anyway we didn't go that route. Both Glendon and I became preachers instead of singers.

195   THE "PALMIST" DAVID

When I was a teenager my church had a radio broadcast (WAPO, Chattanooga) early each Saturday morning. Some young people from church often made it an outing to get up and go to the station. The pastor picked some of us up one morning. On the way, we passed a large sign for a fortune teller, reading "Madam Ruth, Palmist." One of the boys read it aloud, and the preacher corrected him saying, "It is Psalmist not Palmist," and gave Psalmist David as an Old Testament example of the proper pronouncement.

With this joke firmly in his subconscious, the preacher began his radio sermon by saying, "This morning I am reading from the words of Palmist David!" All of us learned a lesson about joking around with the sacred. It could have been funny, but it was serious. Pastors should be careful about what they say to young people.

196   THE TROMBONE SOLO

The music director (Roosevelt Miller) at my boyhood church played several instruments. One Sunday he was on the program to play a trombone solo for the offertory, but he had left his trombone at home. Not to be outdone, he took a microphone in hand and stood behind the stage curtain and proceeded to play his solo using his mouth for the trombone sounds and using the same arm movements as if he had the trombone. It was beautiful.

The audience could not see him clearly, and many did not know he was faking it. The young people knew his secret and later called on him to play his trombone solo at parties when they knew he didn't have the instrument. Each time it brought great happiness. The music director's versatility taught us to use what was at hand and not to make excuses. Each time I am stopped by the absence of something needed to perform a task, I remember the trombone solo and just go ahead and do it anyway!

Mother taught me not to make excuses under any circumstances. Also, at one point in my life as part of 9 months of military readiness training, I could say only three things regardless of the question by certain people: yes, sir; no, sir, or no excuse, sir! Example: Green is it raining, "Yes, Sir!" Why is it raining? "No, Excuse, Sir!" I suppose that prepares one for leadership or to survive as a POW. It was good preparation for ministry, too! Scriptural obedience is without excuse.

197   BROTHER, WHAT ARE YOU DOING HERE?

I spent seven years of my early ministry in the Mountains of West Virginia, traveling the state in youth work. Thirty years later, I was traveling alone late one night through a sparsely populated area of the state on a return trip to Tennessee. The mountain roads were tiresome, and I needed a cup of coffee to stay alert. Nothing was open as I passed through several small towns. Finally, I saw a roadhouse honky-tonk type place that was open. I was thinking that I haven't been in these parts for thirty years so no one will recognize me. I'll just grab a cup of coffee and be on my way.

Feeling a little awkward about entering such an establishment, I reluctantly got out of the car. Someone spoke to me, "Brother Green, what are you doing here?" Somehow after 30 years a former youth camper who had been drinking remembered me. Wide awake now! I kicked my tires and answered, "Just stopped to stretch my legs."

Journeying on, I began to wonder, did I miss God? Was I led to that place to help someone from my past? Did I neglect my duty? Why didn't I just tell the truth and visit with an old friend? Usually when I speak about the Good Samaritan, I tell this story about how I missed an opportunity to guide a friend back to the straight and narrow path. I did not know his name. Was there anything I could do? I said a prayer for him and asked that God send a Good Samaritan. Just as the Priest and Levite, I had passed a wounded man and missed an opportunity and the blessing of obedience. I made a vow never again to miss another opportunity to share the good news.

198   TRIGONOMETRY SMOKES COKE

Several years ago I was driving south on I-75 and picked up a traveler. He had long red hair, a full beard, and carried a small backpack. As he entered my car, for some unknown reason, I said, "Trigonometry smokes coke!" He responded, "I read you loud and clear. You are the first sensible person I have met today." I continued, "What's happening?" His response surprised me.

The traveler told me he was a math professor on sabbatical walking along the highways of America observing the deterioration of the good earth. He said, "If there is a God, he must be really P.O.'d the way mankind has treated the earth." This prompted a long discussion about the reality of God and His creation and ended with God's concern for His greatest creation: man. With this established, I was able to continue the conversation in the area of religious responsibility and personal accountability. It was a profitable discussion. I still am amazed at the way I greeted him, but I am confident God knew he was a mathematician.

I don't encourage others to pick up hitchhikers, but when I travel alone I usually pick up a rider to chat. God always leads. We must step through the open door and listen for the cues to the next step or the next word. This is part of God's plan of getting His message to the world. Everyone who needs the gospel cannot be found in Church on Sunday morning.

199 HENRY LEARNED TO LISTEN

When I first met Henry M. Parks (1922-1995), he was a self-made preacher who had been at the same pastorate for a quarter of a century. He was hungry for more education so I attempted to map out some summer courses at different schools that Henry could take. One was a course in the Philosophy of Religion offered in a Kentucky institution. It was to be taught by a young teacher from Harvard, so I suggested to Henry that he listen and not talk in class.

The young professor opened his first class with an outlandish statement to bait and identify the conservatives or fundamentals in the class. Henry responded loudly, "I don't believe that!" The professor said, "So Mr. Parks you know more about this subject than I do. Perhaps you would like to teach the course." Naturally, Henry declined, but the next time I saw him he clearly understood why I had cautioned him to listen and not to speak. Henry continued to struggle with his studies, learned to listen, and eventually completed Seminary. Everyone was proud of the degree hanging in the Pastor's Study at his church.

200 "PREACHER, YOU AIN'T OLD NO MORE?"

Some years ago I had a gallbladder operation, knee surgery, and had grown a beard. Using a walking stick, I appeared to be much older with my recent sickness and the grey beard. Recovered from the surgeries, the walking stick and beard gone, a young girl at Grandview Baptist Church came up sheepishly and asked, "Preacher, you ain't old no more?" My response, "I'm feeling younger every day." Through the eyes of a child the whole world looks differently. It would be helpful if we all remembered that little bit of information and took a look at the world through the eyes of a child every day. Things would look better.

201   "G W" WAS MORE THAN INITIALS

The Reverend G W (Initials only) Lane (1912-1982), was a father figure to me for 20 years and grandfather to my sons. He was a spiritual man and a great self-made preacher. He could preach anywhere, anytime, or on any subject. His popularity as a preacher created a national radio program and then a national television ministry.

Brother Lane could write a sermon script in one draft and read it on the air, and the audience would believe it was spontaneous. He had a gift, but preaching was not all there was to G W. He traveled a great deal and often in his sermons used the phrase, "I've just come by to tell you!"

On one occasion I observed the man as he received three messages of calamity in the space of a few hours. His measured response, his professional behavior, and his resignation to God's Will touched me. I asked him about the occasion. The response was straight forward, "I have learned that when an event or person is beyond arms reach there is nothing I can do. Why fret about it? I simply turn it over to God." He never let personal limitations or difficulties hinder his commitment to preach the gospel. This was a spiritual legacy passed to both family and friends.

202 AN EFFECTIVE KIND OF COUNSELING

During a thirty-four year pastorate, Henry M. Parks attempted to improve his education. Wanting to be a more effective counselor for his members, he enrolled in a counseling course. Prior to the course he was an effective pastor and dealt directly with the problems of the congregation.

For example, a woman shared with him about the unfaithfulness and drunkenness of her husband. She told him he came home every Saturday night and beat her and that was the reason she could not attend Sunday services at times. Being directive, he told her to get a ball bat and stand at the top of the stairs because men such as her husband only understood force. The next Saturday night she knocked a home run with her husband ending up at the bottom of the stairs and in the hospital. Henry visited the husband and told him, "If you don't straighten up that woman might kill you." He prayed, joined the church, and eventually became an active deacon in the church.

Another example was a similar story. A drunken husband was bringing his buddies home for a tete-a-tete with his wife, but the remedy was different. The pastor told her a "man like that ought to be shot." It was only a figure of speech, but the woman took him literally. The next Saturday night she shot him three times. In the hospital, he was scared. He listened to the same story from Preacher Parks and decided if he didn't straighten up his wife might kill him. He prayed, was baptized, and became an active member of the church.

What is the moral of this story? Brother Parks told me that according to the counseling course he had been doing everything wrong. He said he changed to become a non-directive counselor. Tragically, he said since he changed methods he had not been able to help anybody. "The grunt and punt method of counseling was not direct enough to be effective," he shared sadly. Sometimes it doesn't pay to mess with something that works. As Maj. Gen. Jerry R. Curry, USA (ret.) used to tell me, "Don't fix what ain't broke."

203 WHEN I SEE GOD, I'LL TELL HIM. . .

A letter came from the Texas State Prison requesting books to read from the library. It was from Steve Moran on death row. Since the graduate library did not loan books, I took some personal volumes and sent them to him and asked a friend in North Carolina to send him a box of books.

Later my son, Barton, wrote a book about Steve Moran and his conversion, and I learned that he had killed several women in Texas and was under 13 death sentences. Notwithstanding his criminal past, Steve was hungry to learn all he could about the Christian faith. He wanted to make up for wasted time. I sent him a reading/study plan developed for my students called the Zeta Method for Self-study to guide his reading and making a "learning log."

A letter came from Steve that informed me the date had been set for his execution and that he would not appeal since he was guilty. He returned the books together with a summary/analysis of what he had read since being on Death Row. It was impressive. He assured me that he had read all of them and that many of the men on death row had also read the books. He asked to keep one book, a modern version of The Pilgrim's Progress, because some of the men still wanted to read it. (It was later returned by the Prison Chaplain).

At the close of the letter he thanked me again for my kindness toward him, and expressed good thoughts for the work of the graduate school I had initiated. Steve closed by saying, "In a few days I will meet God. I will not die as other men. I have been saved. I will give my life for crimes committed, but my soul is safe." The letter ended with a profound statement, "When I see God, I will tell him about you."

Steve Moran died by lethal injection without knowing that Barton, who was writing a book about his life, and I were father and son. We never thought to tell him. Perhaps it didn't matter.

Life is short. We should read, live, love, and share with everyone. Tomorrow it may be over. I have thought often about Steve Moran's simple gesture of expressing to God something about my willingness to share a few books. Of course, God already knew the facts, but somehow it gave a different twist to the whole process to see how a young man, converted after a life of crime and condemned to die, would see a simple act of Christian charity. It gave me confidence that small acts of kindness are remembered and surely recorded in the Master Record Book.

Due to some legal conflicts with the secondary people of the story, Barton's book, Hostage from Heaven, about the life and conversion of Steve Moran was never published. The story of the young lady that caused his conversion should be told. It was one of the significant Christian victories of the twentieth century. The facts of his conversion and his efforts to study and learn all he could would be a source of encouragement to many. He crammed for his final exam. I am confident he received a good grade from the Master Teacher.

204 AN OLD SKUNK AND A YOUNG SOLDIER

Traveling to Washington, D.C., during the Vietnam War to intercede for a young service man mistreated because of his Christian faith, God opened a door for me to witness.

Just before catching the plane, my schedule took me to a publisher to review the galley proof of a book on Discipleship. While there an old newspaper was noticed on the floor. Since neatness is a virtue, my decision was to pick up the paper. It had been used to cover an ink spill and was stuck to the floor. In the process, a small piece tore off in my hand. It was a picture of a skunk and a story about a Pennsylvania farmer.

A Pennsylvania farmer had observed an aging skunk for several days. One day the skunk abandoned his old home and dug a new nesting hole. The farmer was intrigued, so he watched. The skunk with great care gathered grass and leaves and lined the inside of the excavation. The old skunk looked around for what was to be his last glance at the world, and then entered the hole. The behavior fascinated the farmer so he waited. When the skunk never came out of the hole, the farmer became curious.

Taking a stick, the farmer punched into the hole. Nothing happened. Finally, he knelt down and raked back the leaves so the skunk could be seen. The skunk did not move; it was dead. The farmer observed that the skunk was old, the teeth were broken, and concluded the skunk could no longer hunt for food and had prepared to die. Reading this story seemed foolish at the time, but God had a reason.

Seated about half way back in the coach section, a young soldier chose the empty seat beside me. As the plane took off, the soldier turned and said, "Sir, I probably won't be alive a year from now; I'm on my way to Vietnam." This matter of fact statement jolted my memory of the skunk story. As the story was shared with the young soldier, his face became thoughtful. The time had come for me to present the claims of Christ. If an old skunk had the awareness and enough sense to prepare to die, surely it would be wise for a soldier going to battle to make preparation to die.

His answer, "Sir, I would if I knew how." The door was wide open. The ABC's of the gospel (All have sinned, Believe on the Lord Jesus Christ, and Confess with your mouth and you will be saved) were presented. The young soldier prayed to receive Christ and went to war prepared to die. God used spilled ink, an old newspaper, a plane ride, and a troubled, but searching heart, to do the work of redemption. All believers should be open to each and every opportunity to share the good news.

205 HOW BIG SHOULD A COW BE?

Some years ago my speaking at a Canadian Church Growth Conference created a discussion about the size of a church. In reviewing my philosophy of growth someone suggested that my view depreciated the large super-church in favor of the small community congregation. The question was asked, "How large should a church be?" My response was, "How large should a cow be?" The questioner responded that he did not know.

The group was asked if they were required to determine the normal size of a cow, how they would go about the process. It was suggested that perhaps one should observe and count some cows to determine the average or normal size. The apparent answer was that most mature cows were about the same size.

My next question was, "What if you owned a cattle ranch and discovered a cow in the pasture that was 25 times larger than all the other cows, what would you do?" A participant answered, "I would get it out of the pasture as quickly as possible before it stepped on some other cows." Could this have relevance for the super-church? If not in the process of becoming an abnormally large church, then soon after -- other smaller congregations in the area may be trampled. This is not the intention of church leadership, but is a logical consequence of super-growth. Everyone wants their church to grow, but normal growth should have some relevance to the local community. What size can the community support without doing harm to smaller churches?

This fact exists. Research demonstrated that in one southern city a large Baptist church brought about the demise of thirteen other small Baptist churches. It is the law of the sea: big fish eat little fish. Notwithstanding the church needs to be large enough to support an effective ministry to a community, the data suggests that small congregations are generally more effective in evangelism and missions. A few super-churches scattered around the United States will not adequately serve the spiritual needs of many thousands of communities.

One should remember that church growth is based on two factors: new converts and new congregations. Gathering members from other churches is attendance building not true growth, academically it is called "transfer growth" but in reality it is not growth of the kingdom. Each growing church should evaluate the "nature" of their growth and be certain that in their zeal to build attendance they are not causing others to suffer loss.

206   READING THE BIBLE AT 2 AM

For years there has been an annual Bible Reading Marathon in the Chapel of Oxford Graduate School. The New Testament is read aloud chronologically by books each November to celebrate both American Education Week and National Bible Society Week. The desire is to demonstrate that the Bible still is relevant to education and has value in family life. The reading begins at 6 PM on a Friday and continues through the night until about 5:30 PM on Saturday. The Campus Chapel is a small English-type church building that seats about 200 people.

During the reading only a few are present, except the reader. On the occasion of the first marathon (1990), a young girl from the local YMCA was reading at about 2 AM (the children from the YMCA always picked a reading time so they can stay up late). The young girl read, "He that believeth and is a Baptist shall be saved, he that believeth not shall be commended." Her mother in the audience tried to stop her and correct the reading, but the little girl kept on reading.

Since she attended the local United Methodist Church, someone jokingly shared with the pastor that according to the scripture read by one of his members, he could never be saved since he was not a Baptist; the best he could hope for was to be commended. Oh, in case you don't know how the verse should read: "He that believeth and is baptized shall be saved, he that believeth not shall be condemned." Who said reading the Bible at 2 AM couldn't be fun!

On another occasion a young boy was troubled with some Bible names in Matthew that he could not pronounce. The person in charge said, "Son, just say steamboat and continue." Those present clearly heard the following:

"1 The book of the genealogy of Jesus Christ, the Son of David, the Son of Abraham: 2 Abraham begot Isaac, Isaac begot Jacob, and Jacob begot Judah and his brothers. 3 Judah begot Perez and Steamboat by Tamar, Perez begot Steamboat, and Steamboat begot Ram. 4 Ram begot Steamboat, Steamboat begot Steamboat, and Steamboat begot Salmon. 5 Salmon begot Boaz by Rahab, Boaz begot Obed by Ruth, Obed begot Jesse, 6 and Jesse begot David the king." --Matthew 1:1-6. Because of this difficulty with Matthew, I recommend that young converts begin reading the New Testament with Mark, the oldest of the Gospels. Mark is presented first in The EVERGREEN Devotional New Testament (Complete Edition). You can find the DNT at the site www.gea-books.com and such sites as Amazon, etc.

207   A SHRINE TO SAINT HOLLIS

Traveling in Peru gathering stories for a magazine, I arrived in Lima the week the Pope declared that several saints were to be taken off the official Vatican list. I searched the streets of Lima seeking someone who could speak English better than I could speak Spanish. Finally, I found a young man about 25 and asked him about the Pope's decision to take certain saints off the list.

The young Peruvian said it didn't matter, that the people could still pray to the defrocked saints, but the church just wouldn't teach the next generation to recognize them. I asked, "Why would you want to continue to pray to a saint who the Pope says is really not worthy?" He responded in effect that the idea of saints was to encourage people to pray; the power was not in the saint, but in the person's faith as they prayed.

That was good reasoning, so I pushed the conversation, "What is a saint, and why does the Church select them?" He explained that a saint was someone who lived so clean and holy that they bypassed Purgatory and went straight to Heaven when they died.

According to that definition and my theology, I was not going to purgatory, I was a saint. I stuck out my hand and said, "I am Saint Hollis!" He appeared frightened, but did not say a word. He just turned and walked away rapidly. After a few steps, he turned and took another look at me, a few more steps, and turned again. I think he believed that I was one of the saints that had been taken off the list and had appeared to him. I observed as he continued toward the local Church, where I assumed he would pray or tell his Priest about seeing Saint Hollis. I have not returned to Lima, but if I do I will take a look on that corner to see if there is a shrine to Saint Hollis.

208 A TOUGH ACT TO FOLLOW

One morning I arrived early for a speaking appointment at a state convention in Oklahoma. The parking lot and the building were packed. I thought they had all come to hear me preach, but it was time for the "annual sermon" and a particular old preacher was scheduled to speak. He spoke with a boldness and flare I had never seen before.

As the old man started, I instantly understood why the people had come. It was going to be the "mother of all sermons." He began, "When the women's dresses got up to the knee caps, I didn't say nothing; but, since the skirts have gotten up to the hubcaps, I'm gonna say something!" And he did! Again and again! For some strange reason the people loved it. I think it was a kind of comic relief not normally found in religious services. He also talked about the evils of "sircuses, carn-eviles, gambling, whisky and watching Red-skillet on the devil box...."

I have always wondered what would have happened if I had arrived late and missed the annual sermon. I guess I would have honestly believed the crowd had come to hear me speak. The old preacher was a tough act to follow, but I had a good crowd. Life does have a few compensations when one is prepared to do his best regardless of competition or circumstance. Many years later an old preacher remembering that day said, "Son, you did well following that mess!"

209   SECRET BALLOT, MY FOOT!

My last pastorate was a rural church in Rhea County, Tennessee. I agreed to speak for a few weeks while the pulpit committee searched for a permanent pastor. I was in the early stage of developing Oxford Graduate School and needed to stay close by, so when the committee asked me to stay 90 days I agreed. At the end of the 90 days the committee still had not found a permanent pastor and asked if I could assume the responsibility for an extended time. I was told this would require a vote of the congregation. At the meeting someone suggested a "secret ballot" and one elderly lady stood with determination, "Secret ballot, my foot, stand and be counted! I'm sick and tired of these secret ballots. If you don't have the courage to publically stand, just don't vote."

Another member asked, Dr. Green, how long can you stay? My answer, "It depends on the growth and demands of my time at the graduate school. I will have to be away one Sunday each month, but I can give the committee a 90 day notice when I need to be relieved. Another brother stood, "I rather have a good preacher three Sundays a month, than a bad one four Sundays." The vote was taken with almost everyone standing. I remained pastor of Grandview Baptist Church for seven (7) years, built a new church valued at $250,000 and paid off the debt before turning the church over to a new minister. I will always remember, Sister Alma and her, "Secret Ballot, my Foot!"

210   I WOULDN'T ATTEND THIS CHURCH

Scheduled to preach in a Georgia church on a rainy day, I was running late. When I arrived, the parking lot was full except for a small section under about three inches of water. Late, I had to park somewhere, so I parked and waded toward the church. The rear door was locked; the side door was locked. I climbed the front stairs and found a door open and entered the sanctuary.

An elderly ladies' Bible class was meeting in the back of the sanctuary, so I sat down on the back row dripping wet. A little lady wobbled up to me and handed me an offering envelope and a Lesson Leaflet. I asked, "Where might the pastor be?" She pointed to the door to the left of the stage. I walked through that door and saw a long hallway. Continuing I heard voices and noticed an open door. Standing outside the Sunday school office, I waited for someone to notice me.

A man jumped up and asked, "How old are you?" I answered. He pointed down the hall and said, "First hall to the right; second door on the left." Opening the door, I bumped into the teacher, a giant economy size lady. The only empty seat was just in front of her. As she taught the lesson, she would lean over the small lectern and deride anyone with an education. I began to wonder why I had been invited to speak.

When the lesson was over, I made my way to the pulpit area. Still no one had spoken to me except to ask my age. As I pondered my prepared sermon, I decided it was not appropriate for the occasion. Taking a new approach, I began my sermon, "If I lived in this community, I would not attend this church!" I told the story of wading in the parking lot, finding the doors locked, and coming in the front door soaking wet.

By the time I completed my story, some began to realize how awkward it must have been for a guest preacher to be treated in the manner I described. Finally, I posed the question, "What if I had been a newcomer to the community looking for a church?" Then I asked, "How would you feel if it were someone you invited?" By the close of the sermon, the deacons were mad, and in a short meeting decided not to give me the normal honorarium.

Two weeks went by, and the Chairman of the Deacons called my home saying, "Dr. Green, you were right. Everything you said was true, and we should have accepted what you said as a rebuke from the Lord. We would like to send you a nice love offering." I told them to put the offering in the next missions drive. I really did not want any connection with that church unless it changed its attitude drastically about visitors. I never heard from them, but a few years later, I dropped past the building and found it empty. I hope they learned their lesson and moved on to bigger and better things, but I have my doubts. When church members behave in a selfish and unconcerned manner toward others, a drastic change in attitude is not the normal outcome. No wonder there are so many small and weak churches.

211   SHOES AND PANTS WERE IN KNOTS

Several young preachers were invited to a big church convention in Birmingham by John D. Smith. He had secured a room with twelve (12) army cots to cut down the costs. During lights out the first night, John came to each cot and prayed for each one of us. We slept well thinking at least there was one person in the world who cared about young preachers.

The next morning we all awoke to reality. During the prayers, John had tied our shoes together, tied knots in our pants, taken our belts out and fastened them to the cots; it was a mess. Somehow the message got through to each one of us that you can be a Christian and still have some fun. It was a good trip, and John D. Smith became a lifelong friend for us all.

212   KNEELING, "DEAR GOD, BLESS . . ."

The first morning everyone rushed off to find breakfast; that is, after they untangled their pants and shoes. I was the last one to leave and finally find a little place to eat, but there were no tables. One large table invited me to join them in time to order. When breakfast came, an elderly man was asked to say grace.

Expecting a simple and quiet prayer, I was shocked to see him get up and kneel down on the floor by the table and pray at the top of his voice for all present including the waitress and the cooks. I think he even prayed for the farmers who raised the chickens that laid the eggs. To say the least, I was embarrassed and steered clear of that bunch at meal times that week.

213   THE PASTOR'S STRIPED SHORTS

Pastor John D. Smith was recovering from a heart attack. He was lounging around in some old pants when he heard his car start. His son, Rusty, was playing "hound bus" in the car . . . turned the key, and it started. It was in reverse and the idle was high, so it began to move backward with Rusty steering from side to side. It went across the lawn, through the hedge, into the flowers, and on to the street. As the car backed down the street, idling just enough to keep it going, John caught up with the car. Stretching over the half-open window trying to reach the key, the button popped on his old work pants. The pants fell and hobbled John. With his red and white stripped shorts shining brightly, he hopped along until he was able to stop the car.

Returning to the parsonage, John said, "Blanche, start packing; we are moving. Every woman on this street has seen my shorts. How can I face them on Sunday morning?" John did make it to church the next Sunday and told the story on himself to the whole congregation to get it behind him. Sometimes on a slow day, I remember John, and a sheepish smile comes to my face. Isn't it good that God made a few special people to make life exciting?

214 HE HAD THREE, BUT HE PREACHED FOUR

I was the Assistant Pastor of a large church with a home spun pastor named John Smith. John was a down to earth guy, mostly self-made. He had little formal education, but was crammed full of common sense and practical know how.

The weakest part of his ministry was his preaching. He had three sermons, but he preached four.

John preached about salvation, living the separated life, or the ministry of the Holy Spirit... or sometimes with great emotion, he preached a little of all three and wept. We called that sermon, "The Ministry of Tears." It was not intended to degrade John, but to acknowledge his compassion and sincere interest in people.

How John ever made it on three sermons can only be explained by the fact that he preached the fourth. People saw his heart and knew he was sincere. His ministry was most effective. He started late in life. He built two churches is his hometown of Chattanooga, Tennessee, and went on to pastor the largest local church in his denomination.

John Smith was truly a God called preacher who communicated the Love of God through life and lip. I was pleased to know and work with him when I was a young man. He organized and built churches in his hometown (a most difficult task). One church in South Carolina loved him so much that when he was ready to retire a committee of men came to John and said, 'If you will retire in our city we will build you a home.' They let John and Blanche pick a corner lot and house plans. The men built the house and gave it to the Smiths debt free. This is the first knowledge of a local church caring so much for a former pastor. Brother John was a special case.

215 THE COOK WILL NOT GET TO HEAVEN

While living in Beckley, West Virginia, I often ate at the Eatwell Café. I would order a steak "extra well done." I remembered looking at meat under a microscope in school and always wanted it cooked well done. On one occasion, the steak came rare. I sent it back to the cook twice. The third time it was returned, I told the waitress to tell the cook that he would never make it to Heaven.

The waitress knew I was a preacher, so she told the cook, "That preacher out there said you would never make it to Heaven." The cook, a kind and gentle man, came to my table somewhat distressed and asked for an explanation. He complained, "You don't even know me. How can you say such a thing?"

The cook was told the Bible said that those who make it to Heaven would hear, "Well done, thou good and faithful servant!" Since I had asked for a well-done steak three times, I assumed he could not hear the words, "Well done;" therefore, I assumed he would not make it to Heaven.

At first he was distressed, and then he smiled. I got a well-done steak. In fact, each time I entered that restaurant after that the waitress would say, "Here comes the preacher; burn one!" I always enjoyed a well done steak and the gentle smile of the cook. Communication is a wonderful thing...when it works.

216 SHE READ ALOUD, "# $ * @ % ^* + #."

A local church in Knoxville where a friend was pastor decided to boycott certain TV programs because of bad language. Someone in the effort made a list of the curse and vulgar words used on the designated programs. The list was printed and passed out in the Sunday morning service to encourage the membership to avoid the particular programs. A hard of hearing lady who forgot her glasses turned to a neighbor next to her and asked her to read the announcement.

Without thinking, the lady began to read loud enough for the hard of hearing woman to understand (of course the whole congregation could hear it as well). She read, "Here are some of the words '*&^#@&^$@!<@' used in recent programs." She kept reading aloud until a lady in the next pew turned around and stopped her. It was all done in an innocent effort to assist another, but the consequences were surprising for the pastor and the congregation.

217 "I JUST GOT TO TELL IT"

Some years ago I visited a pastor friend who had been at the same church about twelve years. His wife was unhappy about the long stay and wanted her husband to take a call to another church. She shared with me her frustration with the same routine each Sunday. She said, "I know everything that is going to be said before it is said. We are in a monotonous rut."

The next morning I was scheduled to speak at the morning worship service. Seated on the platform, I could see the pastor's wife. She mouthed the words for each person as they spoke, even her husband. The offering, the announcements, the special music, the deacon's prayer, she knew each one word for word. At last, I was introduced to speak. Just as I opened my Bible, a little lady on the second row jumped up. Startled, my eyes dropped to the pastor's wife, and she mouthed the very words the little lady said, "I just can't wait; I just got to tell it!"

218 THE BOYS WHO DIED IN THE SERVICE

During a Memorial Day Service at St. Michael's at the Northgate in Oxford, UK, a grandmother attempted to quiet a small boy by saying, "Be still, son, they are reading the names of the boys who died in the service." According to Steven Pix, the program was long, and on the way home the young boy asked, "Grandmother, when did those boys die? Was it in the morning service or the evening service?"

219   NAMES ARE IMPORTANT

In my early ministry during one visit to a small rural church I met a "cat lady." She had nine (9) cats and knew them all by name. They were called Atonic, Alogue, Abolic, Apult, Aract, Alina, Acomb, Astropic, and Erpillar. With so many cats, she was asked, how do you remember their names? Her answer was simple, "All their first names are CAT!" She continued, "If you know their first name, the rest is easy."

I learned a lesson that day. First names are important. Later a psychology teacher reinforced the concept, saying, "Each person has their name tattooed on their chest, remember it because it is important." Then he said, "Protocol requires you to call me Professor Alexander, but you should also know my name." At that moment, he unbuttoned his shirt, opened it wide and written with a magic marker on his chest was, John Dixon Alexander. In my years in public service, as public relations director, pastor, military chaplain, professor in higher education, and publisher I always tried to learn the first name of those with whom I associated. Not nick names or childhood names, but their real, legal first name.

Because of this understanding, I gave my first son the real name, Barton, after my deceased father. Then I gave him a nick name "Barty" because he had red hair and I knew the kids would call him "Red Green." I also hoped as he grew Barty would be shortened to Bart and then as an adult he would be known as Barton. My second son was named Brian Lane after his grandfather. Lane was a special name and I wanted it to be carried forward. As a professional singer, Broadway star, singer, playwright, and director, he is formally known as "Brian Lane Green." Naming a child is important, because names are important!

220 MY FLEA MARKET FUNERAL SERMON

Each January when I take students to Oxford, England, I search for flea market books and English paraphernalia. In 1996 I found a very special translation of the New Testament printed in 1945. Obviously, a translation done in the midst of WWII would have a particular perspective. In fact, it was translated by an Oxford Scholar and was the first work translated directly from the Vulgate Latin and authorized by the Archbishops and Bishops of England and Wales since 1582 when another Oxford Scholar completed his work. What made the finding of this flea market Bible significant was the death of my dear friend and colleague George D. Finigan, EdD, DPhil.

Dr. Finigan had been losing ground for some time with kidney problems, but his heart attack was unexpected. I had to fly from London to Boston to speak at his funeral, but had none of my normal preaching material with me. I had been George's pastor for five years and had ordained him as a deacon, a position he cherished. He always seemed to enjoy my preaching. The question was, how could I prepare a proper sermon that would do honor to George's commitment to Christ?

Reading another flea market find, a book about Dietrich Bonhoeffer, I learned that one of his final days included a devotion from 2 Corinthians 1:17- 22. As I read verse 20 from my flea market Bible, "In him all the promises of God become certain; that is why, when we give glory to God, it is through him that we say our Amen." The German language from the book on Bonhoeffer translated "the final Amen." I had my sermon for George.

George was sure of his salvation; there was no hesitation between "yes" and "no." In Christ, George had his "final Amen." It is amazing what one can find in a flea market. It is wonderful that God is always working to provide what one needs to fulfill spiritual obligations. Such events help keep a perspective on the "final Amen" which will come to us all. Have you checked out a flea market lately? You may be surprised at what you may find.

221 THE ZEBRA HIDE IN MY HOME OFFICE

I have a zebra hide hanging in my home office. It was a gift of Dr. Dewayne Davenport, a missionary to Africa. Dr. Davenport died recently, and at his grave side a young boy came up to me and asked, "Are you family or friend?" My answer was, "Dr. Davenport was my friend."

The energetic young boy continued, "I am sorry that Grandpa is not here to see you; he has gone to a better place." It was so simple and yet so true. Each time I see the zebra hide, I am reminded that my friend is in a better place and that he left a small grandson on earth to carry on his good work. Life does go on.

A zebra died on an African plain and created a talisman that speaks volumes to me. It speaks of missionary commitment, sacrifice, friendship, and of a young lad who clearly understood his grandfather's faith. A friend died... but life and memories continue.

222 THE PHONE BOOTH CALL WAS FOR ME

Many years ago my boss and I were speaking at an Air Force Base. He spoke just before lunch on Executive Stress and said in closing, "If I ever go over the hill, ask if the telephone was ringing when I left."

As we hurried to the cafeteria, the phone in an outside booth was ringing. My boss answered it and said, "Green, it's for you!" Thinking perhaps it was an effort to illustrate his lecture, I picked up the phone. It was for me.

My secretary eagerly wanted permission to do something. Before she was given approval, I asked, "How in the world did you find me?" Her answer was that she knew I was on that particular base and that I would probably eat in the cafeteria. She had called every five minutes from noon until she reached me. It is difficult to get away from "that ringing box," and now we have cell phones everywhere.

Sometimes I wonder about the future of the human race. It is getting a little too fast for me. I feel much like the man that said, "Stop the world! I want to get off!" I think I will enjoy the "long rest" and the opportunity to put my feet in the River of Life in the Heavenly City. Scripture declares, "How beautiful are the feet of them that carry the gospel." The scripture didn't say that one's feet get mighty tired on the journey. However, I truly believe the end is worth the journey!

223 NO AGE DISCRIMINATION

Early in 1987 an elderly gentleman made out an application to Oxford Graduate School. His name was Wallace DePartee, a Yale graduate. The application came at a busy time, and the admissions department was slow in responding to Mr. DePartee. He called for the Head of the School. The call was routed to me. Mr. DePartee was friendly but firm in his dissatisfaction with the slow response to his application. I asked why he wanted to return to graduate school. His answer was classic. "I think the last five years of a man's life ought to be the best, the most productive. I want to write and leave my ideas and lessons learned for the next generation. A doctorate would validate my work and provide credibility for the things I accomplished during my dual career of teaching school and serving a pastorate."

Mr. DePartee was 70 years old but made it clear that he was still young and active. He clearly warned me, "You can't discriminate against me because of my age. I pastor a church, operate three businesses, I baptized six last Sunday, and can run a mile on my toes." Wallace was accepted and made a good student.

When Wallace graduated with his doctorate, he gave me a five-year plan and a ministry budget to support the plan. Five years later, he sent another five-year plan supported by a budget. He became a financial supporter of the graduate school, and at his death, his wife funded a Reading Room at the Study Centre in his honor. She used the balance of the budget from his last five-year plan. Often I remember Dr. Wallace DePartee and his five-year plans. I am reminded that one never gets too old to learn and make a meaningful contribution to family, friends, and society.

I have adopted Dr. DePartee's philosophy. I truly believe that the last five years of one's life should be the most meaningful and productive. With this in mind as I neared retirement from Oxford Graduate School, I initiated in 2002 OASIS UNIVERSITY in St. Augustine (Curepe), Trinidad, WI. Then in 2007, Gail and I incorporated Global Educational Advance, Inc., and initiated a publishing venture, GlobalEdAdvancePress, to make available serious books by strong academic authors. You may purchase good books and understand more clearly our global vision by visiting the website at [www.gea-books.com or www.globaledadvance.org].

224   THE DEACONS HAD A FIGHT

I was lecturing in a National Convention on leadership.
In the course of the class I said something to the fact,
"One who is not willing to be number two is not worthy to
be number one." A pastor in the class came to me after
and asked, "Do you truly believe what you said about being
number two?" I assured him that it was a firm belief. "In
that case, I would ask you to come and be my Assistant
Pastor. I have the largest congregation in my denomination."
I agreed to accept his invitation.

When I moved to assume the position, there was a big
dinner to welcome my family. The pastor placed me between
two large deacons. During the meal they began to argue with
each other about something. When their voice was raised
and it appeared they might come to blows, the pastor said,
"Boys take it outside." To my astonishment they exited the
building. There was lots of noise and banging against the
building. After a few minutes they both retuned disheveled
and distraught to their seats on both sides of me. The
pastor asked, "Did you boys work out your differences?" As
I waited anxiously for an answer, the whole group began to
laugh. It was a set up; it was their initiation for the new
minister. I tried to laugh with them, but the whole episode
was disconcerting to say the least.

225   A MINISTRY IS NOT ABOUT MONEY

At a Church Dinner during National Education Week
honoring the teachers from the congregation, the guests were
discussing life and career, when the husband of an honorees
ask a question of one of the teachers. He was a business
man and asked, "What's a child going to learn from someone
who decided that their best option of making money was to

become a teacher?" To stress his point, he asked another guest; "You're a teacher. Be honest. What do you make?"

The Teacher, who had a reputation for honesty and frankness replied, "You want to know what I make? (She paused for a moment, then began...) "Well, I make kids work harder than they ever thought they could. I make a "C" child feel like an Honor Student. I make kids sit through 45 minutes of class time when their parents can't make them sit for 5 minutes without games, a cell phone, or movie rental.

You want to know what I make? (She paused again and looked at each one at the table) I make kids wonder. I make them question. I make them apologize sincerely. I make them have respect and take responsibility for their actions.

I teach them to write and then I make them write. Keyboarding isn't everything. I make them read, read, read. I make them work in math with a pencil. I make them use their God given brain, not the man-made calculator. I make my students from other cultures learn everything they need to know about English while preserving their unique cultural identity. I make my classroom a place where all my students feel safe. Finally, I make them understand that if they use their gifts, work hard, and follow their hearts, they can achieve their goals in life. (She paused one last time and then continued.)

Then, when people try to judge me by the money I make, with me knowing my ministry to children is not about money, I can hold my head high and pay no attention because they just don't understand the teaching profession.

You want to know what I make? I MAKE A DIFFERENCE! Teaching is...the profession that makes all other professions possible! What do you make besides money, Mr. Business man? His jaw dropped, he went silent. (What kind of a society would this be without TEACHERS who make something out of our children?)

226   A GOOD BAD EXAMPLE

One year in a West Virginia summer youth camp there was trouble in the three boy's cabins on the hill. At breakfast I learned that the three adult counselors for the cabins had left in during the night. It seems they could not control the conduct of the cabin.

What must I do? Observing the boys at breakfast, I noticed one, Truman Smith, who seemed to be the ring leader of the trouble. He was invited to speak to me privately. Thinking he was to be disciplined, he arrived with a bad attitude. We discussed the trouble in the cabins and he said, "Those counselors were wimps." This brought me to the purpose of the meeting. "Truman, you are a born leader. Do you think you could control the conduct in those cabins?" His answer was simply, "Sure!" Then he hesitated and said, "I'm really good for nothing, so I am not sure." My response, "Everyone is good for something." When pressed as to what he was good for, I responded, "You are the best bad example I have ever seen and I am going to preach about you the rest of my life."

Then I reached in the desk drawer and retrieved a STAFF pin. Placing the pin inside his sweater, "This is your authority to discipline those cabins. I know you will do a good job, but you cannot show this pin to anyone but another staff member. Can you do the job without fighting?" Again, his answer was a humble, "Sure."

There was no more trouble from the boys in those three cabins. Truman Smith eventually became a pastor. Adults should be careful how they handle potential leaders among the young people. Those who give the most trouble may actually be born leaders just waiting for an opportunity to demonstrate their potential. At least it was in the case this young man. Truman grew to become an effective pastor.

227   DIALOGICAL PREACHING

In Seminary when I taught Homiletics I remember sharing the point of a sermon was to arouse a spirit of inquiry in the audience and get them involved in internalizing the message. Speaking in rural church in Southern Illinois, I remember an occasion where it actually worked.

It was Sunday morning, a special "community Sunday" when the church was attempting to get new people to attend. During my message I asked several rhetorical questions to get the people thinking about the points in the message. A "first time visitor" stood up after each such question and attempted to provide an answer. At first I was somewhat befuddled, then I remembered my teaching about rhetorical questions and dialogical preaching. I was pleased that I finally received an intelligent response by an audience and not just an emotional one.

At the close of the service the pastor rushed to me and said, "That was the richest man in the community and this is the first time to my knowledge he has attended church. He just didn't understand. I am sorry for the interruptions. My response, "It was not an interruption, it was a confirmation that he was truly listening. He did understand! When one listens and internalizes the message it demands analysis and application. It this case it erupted into a dialogical response. I was pleased and I hope he attends your church regularly in the future. You will finally have a real listener.

228   CALL HIM JOHN, BROTHER

Some years ago I was speaking in a Community Church near Baltimore on the subject of "Living a Separated Life." Each time I made a point that God expected believers to live a clean, separated life an old brother in the back would stand

and say "Call him John, Brother." After a few incidents of
this I became confused trying to figure out what the old man
meant. Finally, it dawned on me that this was a community
church and the congregation included several denominations.
Perhaps this man was an old Methodist who had the doctrine
of Sanctification.

The next time I came to the phrase, "God expects
believers to live a clean and separated life," I continued by
saying the old Methodists called this Sanctification." At this,
the old man jumped up and said "If his name is John, call him
John!" He was coaching me to use the term "sanctification"
instead of describing the results of a sanctified life. It
all came out OK. The old man got me to use the term
"sanctification" and I got the message out that it meant to
live a clean and separated life. We both won!

229   NO EASY FIX

In My last pastorate a deacon died suddenly and his
only son, a teenager, reacted to his father's death with a
show of rage. He could not understand, "Why God took my
daddy?" His mother, a gentle lady, had a hard time handling
his misbehaving. Finally, she came to me with a request,
"Pastor please find a place where James can get some help?"
I located a psychiatric center in Chattanooga that agreed
to take him for observation. The condition was that no one
would visit him for three weeks so the center could do their
preliminary work.

After a few days of observation and three weeks of
therapy, his mother and I visited him. When the counselor
asked in our presence, "What are we going to do about this
temper?" the young man responded, "Can't you give me a shot
for that?" The response was "There is no shot for temper!"
But the young man struck back, "I know there is, because

they gave my dog a shot for his temper!" There was a slight difference in the words, but the young man wanted an easy fix for his problem when there was none available.

Would it not be wonderful, if it were as easy as a "shot" for temper? All attempts to fix flawed behavior in the young are noble efforts. It is not easy, but it is necessary. Pastors, parents and professionals must work together to assist those wounded by tragedy that creates traumatic behavior. It will take both the church and the "community of the concerned" to fix such difficulties. We must find common ground between religion and the social and medical sciences and work together to restore emotional and physical balance to those with psychiatric and behavioral difficulties.

230 THE AUTHOR OF SO TALES IS DEAD

Some years ago Dr. Margaret Sullivan said, "Dr. Green when you die they will say the author of SO TALES is dead! They may say nothing about your educational career." At the time I thought it might be nice since so much about my life and ministry is in the book. Now, I hope that I will be remembered for The EVERGREEN Devotional New Testament. The DNT was a 42 year project to translate NT Greek into a devotional language with two objectives: 1) to determine the original intent of scripture, and 2) to reduce the confusion brought about by misunderstanding the words and phrases. What did the Greek word mean "then" and how can the original intent be expressed "now" in a common language to produce a devotional benefit to the reader.

The devotional rendering is structured to keep believers evergreen and growing. Attending church, with all the benefits, is not sufficient; there should be a daily involvement with the New Testament—the primary rule for direction and control of behavior and a relationship to God and others.

INDEX

ABOUT THE AUTHOR

Hollis L. Green, ThD, PhD, is a Clergy-Educator with public relations and business credentials and doctorates in theology, education, and philosophy. A Distinguished Professor of Education and Social Change at the graduate level for over three decades, Dr. Green is a Diplomate in the Oxford Society of Scholars, and author of 40+ books and numerous articles. He served six years as a member of the U.S. Senate Business Advisory Board and with certified membership in several public relations societies (RPRC, PRSA, and IPRC). He served pastorates in five states, was a denominational official for 18 years, and traveled in ministry and lectured in over 100 countries.

Dr. Green was the founder of Associated Institutional Developers (AID) Ltd., (1974) an international Public Relations and Corporate Consultant Company. He was Vice-President of Luther Rice Seminary (1974-1979), and became the founding President (1981) and Chancellor (1991-2008) of Oxford Graduate School,(www.ogs.edu). As part of a global outreach, Dr Green founded OASIS UNIVERSITY (2002) in Trinidad, W.I. (www.oasisedu.org) where he continues to lecture and teach and assist the administration as Chancellor. In 2004, he assisted in establishing Greenleaf Global Educational Foundation in Colorado to advance issues related to the current needs of society.

In addition to his other endeavors, Dr. Green launched Global Educational Advance, Inc. (2007) (www. gea-books.com or www.GlobalEdAdvance.org) to advance higher education and social change through publishing, curriculum development, instruction, library/ learning resources, and global book distribution with 30,000 distributors in 100 countries. His books and assisting authors in publishing are a logical outgrowth of a fifty-year ministry through education. He serves the author/publisher partnership PRESS as Corporate Chair and Co-publisher with his son, Barton. He continues to travel, speak, teach, write books and work with authors in publishing.

~

Go to *www.gea-books.com*
to order other books by Dr. Green.

www.ingramcontent.com/pod-product-compliance
Lightning Source LLC
Chambersburg PA
CBHW021051090426
42738CB00006B/292